THE SAILING
OF THE INTREPID

THE
SAILING
OF THE
INTREPID

THE INCREDIBLE WARTIME VOYAGE OF
THE NAVY'S ICONIC AIRCRAFT CARRIER

MONTEL WILLIAMS, LCDR USN RET.
AND DAVID FISHER

HANOVER
SQUARE
PRESS

HANOVER
SQUARE
PRESS™

Recycling programs
for this product may
not exist in your area.

ISBN-13: 978-1-335-08103-2

The Sailing of the Intrepid

Hanover Square Press
22 Adelaide St. West, 41st Floor
Toronto, Ontario M5H 4E3, Canada
HanoverSqPress.com

Printed in U.S.A.

I dedicate this book to my family,
the core of everything I do.

To my amazing children—Ashley, Maressa, Montel
and Wyntergrace—watching you grow into the
remarkable individuals you are today fills my heart
with immense pride. My love for you is beyond
words, and I will forever cherish the joy you bring to
my life.

To my grandson Damian, a truly extraordinary soul.
Witnessing your growth is a privilege, and it is with
great pride that I dedicate this piece of the Williams
family legacy to you.

To my grandson Kai, your presence is such a gift to
our family, and I am overjoyed to have you with us.

And to my beloved wife, Tara—who is the heart and
soul behind my every endeavor. Your unwavering love
and support are what propel me every day.

As the eagle, perched on a lofty crag scans
the horizon for any foe

That might molest her young, in the nest—
As the fawn is the charge of the doe—

So, this giant vessel of sturdy steel,
Hovers near on the face of the deep

A haven for its myriad of flying men,
as their trysts with death they keep.

May the God, whose presence o'er shadows us all,
Whose voice can command the deep,

Bless each precious son on the INTREPID,
and each one in safety keep.

—Elanore A. Atha

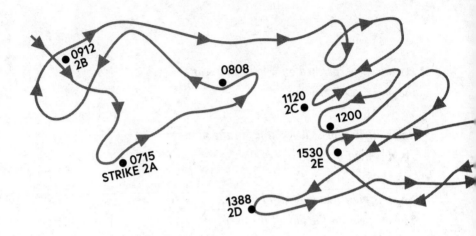

USS INTREPID CV-II
OPERATION CATCHPOLE
Track Chart at Truk Is., Feb. 16–17, 1944

Torpedoed at 0011—2/17— Zone + 12 Time
at Lat. 7°-23'N, Long. 153°-32'E
on 2/16 Strikes Launched: 2A at 0715
                            2B at 0912
                            2C at 1120
                            2D at 1388
                            2E at 1530
                            2F at 1717

Torpedo Hit Starboard Quarter AFT
Rudder Jammed Hard to Port-No Steering
Ship Uncontrollable, Going in Circles.
Two Destroyer-Escorts Put Tow Lines
Aboard, Course Taken 090° True.

INTREPID'S TRACK CHART AT TRUK ISLAND
16–17 February 1944 Operation CATCHPOLE

The Strikes launched on 2/16, beginning
at 0715 hours to 1717 hours.
The Ship torpedoed at 0011 of the 17th.

Originally hand-drawn by Anthony F. Zollo, Sr.
Reproduced by Natasa Hatsios

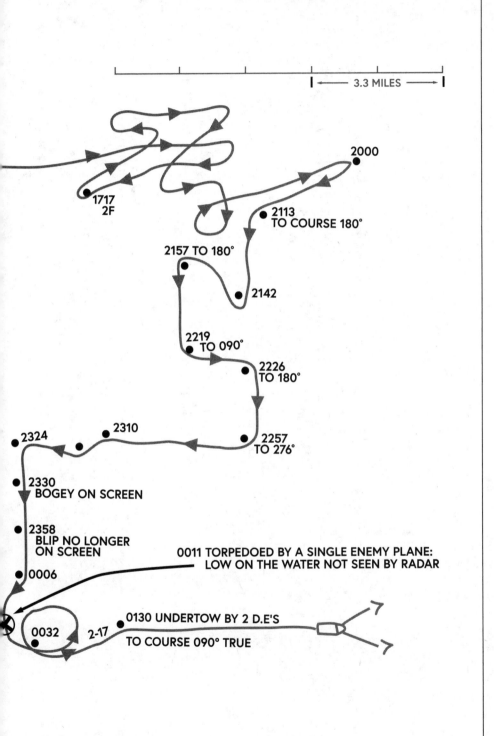

3.3 MILES

2000

1717
2F

2113
TO COURSE 180°

2157 TO 180°

2142

2219
TO 090°

2226
TO 180°

2310

2324

2257
TO 276°

2330
BOGEY ON SCREEN

2358
BLIP NO LONGER
ON SCREEN

0011 TORPEDOED BY A SINGLE ENEMY PLANE:
LOW ON THE WATER NOT SEEN BY RADAR

0006

0032

2-17

0130 UNDERTOW BY 2 D.E'S
TO COURSE 090° TRUE

FOREWORD

THE USS *INTREPID* has been synonymous with the Fisher family for 50 years. Our association with this storied aircraft carrier began in the late 1970s when my late uncle, Zachary Fisher, learned that after its decommissioning in 1974, *Intrepid* was to be scrapped, and lost forever. The son of Russian immigrants and a patriot in every sense of the word, he believed that this historic ship needed to be saved from this unceremonious end, and preserved so its story could be told to future generations.

Working with the Navy and the City of New York, he began the gargantuan effort to save *Intrepid*, bring it to New York, and convert it into a floating museum. After teaming up with legendary journalists and war correspondents Tex McCrary and Michael Stern, and using millions of dollars of his own money, he made a deal with then Mayor Ed Koch to renovate a pier at the west side waterfront of the Hell's Kitchen district that this museum could call home.

After years of working through government bureaucracy and overcoming one obstacle after another, final arrangements were made, and in November 1981, *Intrepid* sailed one final time into New York Harbor, to be permanently moored at its new official address, Pier 86 and the Hudson River. I was fortunate enough to join my uncle for the last sail, a cold, rainy day, and as I wandered her decks, I could almost hear the voices of those sailors who served the ship so gallantly.

Zachary Fisher had brought the *Intrepid* a long way, but he knew that the work was just beginning. He oversaw a massive renovation to make it people-friendly, and he and his associates worked feverishly to secure warplanes, uniforms, and other artifacts that would make up the museum's exhibits, and ensure that each phase of *Intrepid*'s service was represented, including space exploration.

This massive undertaking finally concluded, and in early 1982, the Intrepid Air, Sea and Space Museum officially opened. "The lady who spilled the blood so the other Lady in the harbor could hold the torch" proudly took her place as New York City's newest landmark.

My uncle passed away in 1999, but the impact from *Intrepid* has grown over the years and has been undeniable. When the *Intrepid* opened, the surrounding area was marred by crime, drugs, and prostitution due to years of neglect and a bad economy. *Intrepid* began gentrification of what is now a vibrant neighborhood with development continuing today. It also led to the rebirth of the waterfront, and today the museum is bordered by the Hudson River Park and a revitalized cruise ship port. But perhaps just as important is the number of family initiatives it spawned, aimed at improving the lives and quality of care for our wounded soldiers, veterans, and their families. Notable among them are the Intrepid Fallen Heroes Fund, which built two state-of-the-art rehabilitation centers—the Center for the Intrepid in San Antonio, which provides physical rehabilitation due to the horrific nature of the wounds suffered by our troops, and the National Intrepid Center of Excellence at Walter Reed in Bethesda, which employs the latest innovations in treating the signature wounds of the war on terror, posttraumatic stress disorder and traumatic brain injury.

The Fisher House Foundation was founded in 1990 when my uncle learned that families of our wounded, sick, and injured service members had no affordable place to stay while their loved ones received treatment. Fisher House builds comfort homes for these families to stay in for no charge for as long as they need to. To date, Fisher House has welcomed over 500,000 guest families, saving them over $610 million in travel and lodging, and will open house number 100 early in March 2025. Both benefit from a public/private partnership with the Department of Defense (DoD) and the Department of Veterans Affairs (VA) that spans three decades.

The story of the USS *Intrepid* is, perhaps, one of the most compelling of any naval vessel that sailed under the flag of the United States of America. Commissioned in 1943, this *Essex*-class aircraft carrier was the 11th carrier built. It became known as "the Fighting I" because it sustained multiple Kamikaze attacks and a torpedo hit but kept coming back. Two hundred seventy brave sailors and naval aviators gave their lives serving on her decks or in the skies above her.

Intrepid served in some of the most pivotal battles in the Pacific during World War II. After her service, she became one of NASA's primary recovery vessels during the Mercury and Gemini space programs. After a multimillion-dollar retrofit, *Intrepid* was able to launch and land jet planes, and then did three deployments to Vietnam. As a matter of fact, a young naval aviator named John McCain was one of those who flew from her flight deck.

But the story of *Intrepid* is not just the battles she fought in—it is about the men and women who served aboard her. It is a story of selfless service and sacrifice, of devotion to duty and patriotism. I can think of no one better to tell their story than Montel Williams.

Most people remember Montel Williams as a journalist and television personality. But the Montel I know understands service and sacrifice firsthand, having served 17 years in both the Marine Corps and the Navy, and another 5 years in the reserves. For the last 15 years, I have had the privilege of working with him to improve the lives of our active duty and veteran communities, and those of their families—especially in combating the unseen wounds of war, posttraumatic stress disorder, and traumatic brain injury. He serves on the Fisher House Foundation Board of Trustees, and he continues his service to this nation in a variety of ways, bringing the same passion he has brought to everything else he does. He's a veteran who didn't walk away from his brothers and sisters. I can think of no one as uniquely qualified to tell the story of this proud ship.

Ken Fisher
Co-chairman, Intrepid Museum
Chairman, Fisher House Foundation

INTRODUCTION

"DON'T GIVE UP the ship." These were the dying words of Captain James Lawrence, in command of the frigate USS *Chesapeake* against the Royal Navy frigate *HMS Shannon* in the bloodiest sea battle of the War of 1812. Although *Chesapeake* lost the fight and Lawrence his life, these words were emblazoned on a flag flown on Commodore Oliver Hazard Perry's flagship in the decisive U.S. Navy victory over the British in the Battle of Lake Erie in 1813. For many decades the original flag was displayed in Memorial Hall at the U.S. Naval Academy, inspiring generations of U.S. Naval Officers, particularly those who served in command positions during World War II.

Although USS *Intrepid (CV-11)* suffered a debilitating hit from a Japanese aerial torpedo, her commanding officer, Captain Thomas Sprague (USNA '17), was not about to give up his ship. A hit in a ship's "Achilles' Heel," impairing the rudder, has led to the loss of more than a few major warships that might otherwise have survived, including the German battleship *Bismarck* in the North Atlantic and the Japanese battleship HIEI at Guadalcanal. Barely able to control his ship, a potential sitting duck for Japanese torpedo bombers and submarines, Sprague would need all his decades of experience to get his ship out of harm's way, relying on the sound advice of other key officers and enlisted leaders. Especially critical was the intensive preparation of his crew in "damage control," something that by World War II the U.S. Navy did better than any other navy in the world, and still does today.

From the very beginning, two themes run through the history of the U.S. Navy—ingenuity and heroism. In the American Revolution, the fledgling Continental Navy took on the British Royal Navy, the largest and most capable navy in the world, in this case requiring more heroism than ingenuity. The story of the first *USS Intrepid* during the First Barbary War is an example of both extraordinary ingenuity and heroism. By the War of 1812, American ingenuity produced frigates that were the technological marvel of the era, superior to any other frigates in the world. By the Civil War, American ingenuity on both sides in ironclads, mines and submarines changed the nature of naval warfare around the globe. At the beginning of the 20th Century, the U.S. Navy actually designed the first "dreadnought" battleship before the *HMS Dreadnought*. In this book you will see abundant examples of both ingenuity and heroism.

The Sailing of the Intrepid was initially about heroism, fighting fires and flooding, saving wounded and trapped shipmates. Ingenuity is what would find the solution to controlling the ship and getting her back to Pearl Harbor for repairs, sparing her the fate of four of the first six U.S. aircraft carriers to fight in the first year of war in the Pacific. It is also worth noting that *Intrepid* was authorized, funded and laid down before the attack on Pearl Harbor, in anticipation of the outbreak of war, but still almost too late.

Intrepid would be repaired and go on to serve in the Pacific in the last year of the war, with great valor and significant cost, suffering yet surviving more hits by Japanese kamikaze suicide planes than any other aircraft carrier. The instances of heroism in this period abound, such as the African-American gunners refusing to take cover, firing on an incoming kamikaze to the bitter end, because they refused to let their shipmates down.

This story is told from the perspective of those who were there in the fight to save their ship, serving as an inspiration to the U.S. Navy today. It also serves as a reminder to the reading public of the valor and sacrifice of the U.S. Navy in defending our freedom in the past, present, and what it may yet again be called to do in a dangerous and uncertain future.

Carlos Del Toro, 78th Secretary of the Navy

THE SAILING
OF THE INTREPID

PROLOGUE

ON THE MOONLIT night of February 16, 1804, the Turkish-rigged ketch *Intrepid* rode a gentle breeze into heavily guarded Tripoli Harbor, sailing gracefully under the suspicious eyes of shore batteries and gunboats. More than 100 of the pasha's cannon were primed and aimed at the small ship, protecting the captured American warship *Philadelphia*, a frigate that was taken months earlier by Barbary pirates.

Several ragtag crewmen were visible on deck, working the small merchant ship into the harbor. But another 75 men armed with swords, knives, axes, and pikes hidden behind *Intrepid*'s railings or crouching belowdecks maintained absolute silence. A brief gust ruffled her two canvas sails, the familiar patter that had comforted sailors for 3,000 years. Within minutes they would launch an audacious surprise attack— carrying with them the prestige and the economic fortune of the young American nation. Not since General Washington himself had led his men across the treacherous Delaware River in the legendary Christmas night attack on the Hessians at Trenton almost three decades earlier had American troops risked such a daring raid.

Their mission was clear: board *Philadelphia* and burn it down to its timbers. If this attack succeeded, they would return home as heroes; if it failed, they would die.

Pirates sailing from the Barbary States of Morocco, Tunis, Algiers, and Tripoli had ruled the Mediterranean for centuries, demanding tribute, capturing and holding sailors for ransom or selling them into slavery. Prior to the Revolution, ships from the colonies had sailed the Mediterranean under protection of the British flag, but that had ended with independence. The need to defend American ships from these pirates had led directly to the creation of the United States Navy in 1794. As Thomas Jefferson had warned years earlier, "Our trade . . . to the Mediterranean is annihilated unless we do something decisive."

In 1801, frustrated by the slow pace of peaceful negotiations, Tripoli's pasha, Yusuf Qaramanli, declared war on the United States. In the ensuing years, there had been several minor confrontations. But in October 1803, the frigate *Philadelphia*, second in size only to the *Constitution* in the Mediterranean Squadron, had run hard aground on an uncharted reef and been captured by Tripolitan gunboats. Its 307-man crew had been taken hostage. Soon to be renamed *Gift of Allah*, *Philadelphia* was anchored only 100 yards offshore in Tripoli Harbor, a humiliating symbol of American impotence in that part of the world—and her cannon now a potential danger to merchant shipping as long as she remained afloat.

Philadelphia had to be destroyed.

Commodore Edward Preble, commander of the Mediterranean Squadron, warned, "I shall hazard much . . . it will undoubtedly cost us many lives, but it must be done." It seemed like a suicide mission; somehow a ship had to sneak into the heavily guarded harbor and maneuver close enough to the frigate to set her afire.

American frigates and schooners were so well-known to the pirates, Preble added, they would instantly be recognized and repulsed. If the mission were to succeed, a decoy would be needed.

Weeks earlier, Preble's *Constitution* had chased and captured a Tripolitan bomb ketch—a snug warship designed to attack land targets, equipped mostly with elevated mortars rather than cannon—called the *Mastico*. The ship, sailing to Constantinople flying a Turkish flag, was reported to have been carrying a cargo of soldiers and female slaves. Ironically, *Mastico* had been one of the ships that had captured *Philadelphia*.

Mastico was a new ship, built in France in 1798 by Napoleon in preparation for his Egyptian campaign, then sold to Tripoli. It had little real value—as a prize, it was barely worth $1,800—but it easily could be disguised as a North African merchantman, and it was large enough to carry a raiding party.

The commodore gave the ship a new name: *Intrepid*. It was the perfect name. *Intrepid*, a word rooted in the French *intrépide*, meaning extremely brave and bold and showing no fear of dangerous situations. According to Webster, synonyms include *courageous, valiant, fearless,* and *valorous,* and it "aptly describes anyone . . . who ventures boldly into unknown territory." The name quite accurately fit the mission.

Preble put 25-year-old Lieutenant Stephen Decatur in command of the ship. He was a popular choice. Charismatic, handsome, and resourceful, Maryland-born Decatur was the romantic image of a dashing young officer of the new American Navy. Men wanted to sail with him, and women were said to swoon in his presence. Decatur had been in command of the schooner *Enterprise*, which had assisted Preble's flagship in *Mastico*'s capture.

The attack was meticulously planned: the what-ifs were raised and debated, and precautions were taken. Flying English colors, *Intrepid* would sail into the harbor at night. The six or seven men working on deck would be dressed in native Maltese clothing. The rest of the crew would remain hidden until the last possible moment. An Arabic-speaking pilot would shout for assistance from the guards; he would claim the ship was carrying livestock for the British troops on Malta and had suffered serious damage in heavy storms. Both anchors were gone. Could they tie up to *Philadelphia* for the night?

After making fast to the frigate, the attackers would clamber aboard, overwhelm the outnumbered guards, ignite combustibles throughout the ship, and, ordered Preble, then "make your retreat good."

Storms delayed the attack for five days. *Intrepid* lay well offshore. The men crammed on board suffered badly, forced to eat rotting food and deal with sickness, rats, vermin, and boredom. The superstitious among them called the delay an omen and claimed the mission was doomed. Only Decatur's resolve held the crew together.

The weather finally cleared on the 16th; the order was given: tonight! Decatur planned to sail into the harbor under the cover of night, but the ketch seemed too anxious; it caught the winds and threatened to arrive before sundown.

Decatur ordered buckets and ladders tied astern as drags, successfully slowing her progress.

Intrepid entered the harbor casually, a working ship making port. Guards welcomed her warily. Their lives depended on protecting *Philadelphia*. At the slightest provocation, they would blow the small ship into history. The pilot's voice cut into the night: "We are damaged. We have lost our anchors. We need assistance."

Questions were asked and answered. *Intrepid* bobbed patiently as the guards made their decision. Decatur lay flat and silent on the deck, looking up into the great bowl of stars that filled the night sky. Suddenly, there was movement on *Philadelphia*. Voices were raised. Orders were shouted in a language he did not understand, yet he dared not raise his head. Minutes later, *Philadelphia* lowered a rowboat.

In response, *Intrepid* also put a small boat in the calm water. A hawser was exchanged. The ketch's small crew began hauling on the line, bringing it alongside the frigate. Decatur's men waited, waited, waited as their ship drew closer. Close enough for a lookout on *Philadelphia* to see *Intrepid* still had its anchors—and to see the raiding party. His warning triggered the battle: "Americanos! Americanos!"

Incredibly, Decatur waited several more seconds as his ship drifted closer. When it finally reached the warship, he gave the order: "Board!"

Decatur led the attack; grabbing hold of a forechain, he pulled himself onto the deck. His men followed, swarming onto the boat, climbing over the rails, crawling through the gun ports. In an instant, as a member of the raiding party later described, "like cluster bees . . . every man was on board the frigate."

Rather than fighting, most of the outnumbered, terrified Tripolitans fled for their lives, jumping over the starboard rail, swimming to shore. About 20 brave souls stood and fought, but they had little chance. Within minutes they lay dead or dying on the bloody deck. Just one of Decatur's men was injured, and only slightly.

It took no more than 10 minutes to gain control of the ship. Decatur shouted commands: the bodies were thrown overboard; combustibles were placed throughout the ship, in storerooms, in the cockpit, across the deck, and in the gun room.

On shore, Tripolitan guards in the fort had been alerted; they manned their cannon and began firing pistols wildly and harmlessly. Orders were given to do . . . to do something. But it was far too late. The attack was a complete surprise. The defenders had no means to repulse it.

Decatur ordered the fires set. After using lanterns to light three-inch candle fuses, the men scrambled over the sideboards for safety. Decatur was the last man to leave the blazing *Philadelphia*. Dark smoke poured out of every opening. Then flames rose triumphantly high into the air, climbing the mastheads. The ship's cannon, lit by the flames, fired aimlessly into the night, a dying cry, then tumbled into the sea.

Intrepid pushed off, the dense smoke screening its escape. Oars were manned as the crew attempted to row free, but the inferno sucked it back as if trying to swallow it whole. Men grabbed poles, ready to push away from the burning wreckage if necessary. Decatur put small boats in the water, and they towed her out of the harbor until they caught the wind that filled the sails. *Intrepid* was underway, the burning hulk of a once great warship lighting their path through the night.

The defenders in the fort began firing. One cannonball passed straight through *Intrepid*'s topgallant sail but did no damage. Small arms fire riddled her sides, but no one was hit.

Philadelphia burned through the night, its smoking remains drifting to the shore. And with it went any lingering doubts about the grit or resiliency of the young nation, America—or the ability of its rapidly growing Navy to wage war across the world.

The mission had been a complete success. British Admiral Lord Nelson purportedly declared it "the most bold and daring act of the age." Pope Pius VII was equally amazed, stating, "The United States, tough in its infancy, had done more to humble and humiliate the anti-Christian barbarians on the African coast in one night than all the European states had done for a long period of time."

The name *Intrepid* had been burned into naval history.

Stephen Decatur emerged from the affair a national hero; months later, his reputation grew to almost mythical proportions when he confronted the Tripolitan captain who had mortally wounded his brother. In hand-to-hand fighting, he barely escaped being stabbed in the heart, then shot the much larger man point-blank in his face. His exploits on the Barbary Coast and during the War of 1812 made him an enduring symbol of American naval power and a wealthy and beloved Washington figure.

Intrepid fared less well. After serving briefly as a hospital ship, she was fitted out as an infernal "floating volcano," to be loaded with explosives, sent into the enemy fleet anchored in Tripoli Harbor, and blown up. Her volunteer crew consisted of a dozen men, among them Midshipman Henry Wadsworth, whose nephew was the renowned poet Longfellow. They were to wait till the last possible minute, light the fuses, then flee to safety on small boats.

On September 4, *Intrepid* once again sailed into Tripoli Harbor; this time the guards were alert. Before the 15-minute fuses could be lit and an escape made good, shore batteries opened up. *Intrepid* was hit and literally blown apart. There were no survivors. The first *Intrepid* lived in history.

Seventy years later, the second *Intrepid*, a 170-foot experimental torpedo ram, was launched in Boston. The self-propelled torpedo had only recently been invented, and navies around the world were designing ships to take advantage of its unique and dangerous capabilities. *Intrepid* was an iron-hulled steamer, built as the Navy was completing its transition from "stick and string," masts and sails, to fully steam-powered ships. Although the *Intrepid* was the Navy's first ship capable of firing the new weapon, after several months of trials, it became apparent this *Intrepid* had little value as a warship; instead, it spent almost a decade rusting in navy yards before being sold as scrap in 1892.

The third *Intrepid* was launched in 1904. Designed to turn landsmen into seamen, it was a bark-rigged sailing ship that served mostly as a training ship before being sold in 1921. After being used by the Hawaiian Dredging Company as a barge, she was reacquired by the Navy at the beginning of World War II, serving as a sludge removal barge at Pearl Harbor.

Ironically, YSR-42, as she had become known, was tied to a dock in 1943 when the fourth *Intrepid*, one of the mightiest warships ever built, sailed into the harbor on her way to combat in the Pacific and eased past the barge without recognition.

This is the story of that fourth *Intrepid*, a massive aircraft carrier that was about to embark on one of the most unusual voyages in the annals of modern naval warfare.

ONE

"A LITTLE BIRD learns to fly with perfect ease," noted the *Tacoma Daily News* during the unusually warm October of 1903. "Why can't men fly too?"

That question had tantalized mankind throughout recorded history: Why can't man fly? The secret was right there, right in front of them, as birds of every description lifted easily off the ground and soared gracefully through the heavens in controlled flight. How was that possible?

Dreams of manned flight had been a wellspring of fantasy, from the Greek mythological figure Icarus, who died flying too close to the sun, to Jules Verne's *From the Earth to the Moon*. The genius Leonardo da Vinci had studied birds and sketched hundreds of fantastical flying machines. Many had tried, but no one had been able turn the fantasy into reality.

Beginning in 1783, when the Montgolfier brothers first sent a sheep, a duck, and a cockerel aloft, untethered hot air balloons had given a few brave men the glorious sensation of flight, lifting them a thousand feet into the air to drift capriciously wherever the winds chose to take them. During the American Civil War, balloons had been used to rise above the battlefield to scout enemy positions, giving a hint of the miracles that were possible.

Countless serious efforts to solve the secrets of controlled flight had been made by men using crafted wings or complicated mechanical contraptions. Every one of them had failed. No one dared guess how many men had died or been grievously injured in dangerous attempts.

Among those seeking to master gravity at the beginning of the 20th century was the esteemed director of the Smithsonian Institute, 69-year-old professor Samuel Pierpont Langley. Langley was a brilliant man, one of America's leading physicists, astronomers, and inventors. In addition to discovering the effect of sunspots on earth's atmosphere, he invented the most accurate instrument for measuring temperature as well as the device used to time railroad signals. But Sam Langley's true passion was flight. He had convinced the federal government to fund a spacious laboratory in Smithsonian Castle on the National Mall, and there he had built a wooden machine 60 feet long with 48-foot-wide wings. According to his plan, "The Buzzard," as he named his flyer, would be catapulted by springs or dynamite into the air from tracks laid on the roof of a houseboat in the Potomac River. Then, "assisted by its gasolene motor," it would continue its powered flight.

The Buzzard's first attempt at sustained controlled flight took place on October 7, 1903. Professor Langley's assistant, Charles M. Manly, was at the control arm. At just after noon, reported the *Washington Star*, the "car" was launched. The "mechanical bird . . . took to the air fairly well. The next instant the big and curious thing turned gradually downward," until "all was wreck and ruin." Langley's invention had traveled about 100 yards before crashing into the river.

Professor Langley made two attempts at independently controlled flight. Both failed, and Manley had to be pulled out of the river. Although the Smithsonian later put his craft on display, identifying it as "the first man-carrying aeroplane in the history of the world capable of sustained free flight," the Buzzard was a dismal failure.

Slightly more than two months later, December 17, on the soft sands of windy Kitty Hawk, North Carolina, experienced glider pilots Orville and Wilbur Wright created a worldwide sensation when their motor-powered heavier-than-air Flyer lifted 10 feet into the air from rails and soared 120 feet. It remained airborne for 12 seconds. The brothers flew three more times that day, the first sustained, controlled powered flights in history. The United States government, recognizing the importance of their feat, invited them to Washington to discuss the future of American aviation.

Surprisingly, the Wright brothers' invention was viewed more as a novelty than an extraordinary machine that would transform the world. For example, a representative of Brooklyn's Coney Island amusement center offered the brothers $10,000 to make their next flight from its Luna Park.

Technological advances came slowly. When a British newspaper offered a large prize for the first flight from London to Manchester, for example, the satirical magazine *Punch* responded by offering a similar prize for a flight to the moon.

Aeroplanes, much like the newfangled automobiles, were a delightful diversion, perfect for entertaining awed carnival crowds. Air races and shows featuring daredevil stunts were all the rage as biplanes achieved speeds of up to 66 miles per hour. Everyone agreed aeroplanes, or, as Americans were beginning to refer to them, airplanes, were amazing to watch, an extraordinary feat for mankind, but no one was quite certain exactly how practical they were.

Except, perhaps, the military. Airplanes offered the possibility of scouting enemy positions and observing maneuvers from a safe distance. The Army Signal Corps bought the military's first plane in 1908, paying the Wright brothers $25,000 for a two-seat Model A Flyer, with a $5,000 bonus if it exceeded 40 mph.

Discovering the size and disposition of enemy ships was especially enticing for the United States Navy. That intelligence would provide a huge advantage for its mighty battleships. The United States Navy began training pilots in 1910 and a year later purchased its first plane for experimental purposes. The problem was that the Navy's mission was controlling the seas and no one had yet figured out how to take off from a ship at sea. Even the Wright brothers believed it was far too dangerous.

But engineer Eugene Ely disagreed—and was willing to risk his life to prove it could be done. On land, Ely was a noted speed demon, a racing car driver, but in 1910 he taught himself to fly and became determined to do something no one had done before—fly an airplane off the deck of a ship at sea. It was generally agreed such a feat was impossible, but if it could be done . . .

While officially the Secretary of the Navy refused to sub-sidize such a foolhardy effort, he permitted an 83-foot-long sloping ramp to be constructed over the deck of the scout cruiser *Birmingham*. The conversion was paid for by an anon-ymous aviation enthusiast.

On November 14, 1910, Ely's Curtiss Model D Pusher was lifted aboard the *Birmingham* in Hampton Roads, Virginia. The ship was delayed leaving port, so when a squall threat-ened to force the experiment to be postponed, Ely donned his football helmet and homemade flotation device, revved his engine, and rolled down the ramp of the still-anchored ship, into the air. Almost instantly, the plane dropped beneath the bow; spectators gasped, fearing disaster. But history was a matter of inches. The Pusher's propeller tips churned up Chesapeake Bay, the salt spray briefly blinded Ely, and then magically the wings caught the wind and the plane rose tri-umphantly into the air.

"The aeroplane left the vessel like a gull dipping into the water for a fish," a naval observer aboard the *Birmingham* reported, "then arose and soared away . . . It showed con-clusively that an aeroplane can be launched from the deck of a warship as claimed and that the aeroplane can be made a valuable adjunct to the navy. It was one of the most beautiful sights that ever occurred, I believe."

Although Ely's plane was equipped with pontoons, it flew almost four miles and settled on the sands of Willoughby Beach.

Two months later, Ely once again made history, landing his flimsy machine on a wooden deck constructed on the cruiser *Pennsylvania*, then anchored in San Francisco Bay. As thousands of spectators screamed in fear, the hook he had attached to the bottom of his Pusher caught hold of ropes held taut by 50-pound sandbags. The plane came to an abrupt—but safe—halt 25 feet from where he touched down.

Ely had done it; he had proved that an airplane could take off and land on the deck of a ship, a feat that experts had firmly pronounced impossible. "Aeroplanes Will Scout and Fight in Future Naval Warfare" declared the *San Francisco Call*.

All the navies of the world took notice.

On April 26, 1943, only a few miles from the site of Ely's first takeoff, a small group gathered at the vast Newport News Shipbuilding and Dry Dock Company to witness a ritual that has been performed since mankind first took to the seas more than 5000 years ago, the christening of a great warship.

"Openings to the water I stopped," wrote an ancient Babylonian describing the ceremony ensuring his ship would be favored by the Gods, "I searched for cracks and the wanting parts I fixed; three sari of bitumen I poured over the outside; to the Gods I caused oxen to (be) sacrificed."

Due to wartime security and travel restrictions, only about 100 people had been invited to this ceremony. Earlier that morning, the new ship had tasted water for the first time, as the graving dock, the dry basin in which she had been built, was opened and the waters of the James River flowed in and gently lifted her off a construction platform.

At precisely 9:15, as a golden sun perhaps symbolically eased from behind a dark cloud, Mrs. Helen S. Hoover, the wife of Vice Admiral John Hoover, stood on a raised spon-

Helen S. Hoover, the wife of Vice Admiral Hoover, christening *Intrepid. Collection of the Intrepid Museum. Gift of Mrs. William H. Hoover. P2009.13.09*

sor stand and declared, "In the name of the United States, I christen thee *Intrepid*."

Embracing all the joy of the moment, she swung a bottle of champagne against the mammoth hull—and missed it. She swung once again—and missed a second time. After some nervous laughter, on her third attempt, she smashed the bottle into pieces and was doused by a glorious spray as the relieved observers cheered.

In this way, the United States Navy had welcomed warships to the fleet since October 1797, when one of its six founding captains, James Sever broke a bottle of Madeira wine over the bowsprit of the USS *Constitution*, Old Ironsides, as she "commenced a movement into the water with such steadiness, majesty and exactness as to fill every heart with sensations of joy and delight."

The red wine symbolized blood, harkening back to a time centuries earlier when some civilizations had appeased the Gods with a human or animal sacrifice.

The invocation, a prayer for the welfare of the *Intrepid* and the men who would sail her, was delivered by Chaplain Clinton Neyman, who dedicated the ship to the cause of freedom and justice, asking, "May it serve worthily in the grim but righteous task in which our nation is engaged." His solemn words were mostly drowned out by the din of workers riveting and banging and cranes delivering metal plates on the adjacent building ways. World War II was being won in America's shipyards and factories, operating 24 hours every day, and there was no time to pause for ceremony.

Intrepid was among the mightiest warships ever built. She was the third of a new class of fast carriers, the *Essex* class, designed for the island-hopping campaign that would lead, eventually, to the inevitable invasion of Japan. The modern aircraft carrier was arguably the most complex machine ever designed or built; it was a floating fort, requiring a crew of 3,000 men or more for it to function. It was capable of arming, launching, retrieving, and even repairing a hundred warplanes while defending itself in combat against enemy surface ships, submarines, and aircraft.

Intrepid had been conceived in 1940, as war was spreading across Europe and Asia. Congress finally had been convinced that taking the war to the enemy required a large fleet of air-craft carriers. The *Essex* class, which was designed to carry substantially more aircraft than existing carriers, was made possible only after existing treaties with Japan had been dis-solved in 1936. These ships were marvels of modern tech-nology. They were longer, wider, and much heavier than the previous *Yorktown* class. They would revolutionize naval war-fare, supporters promised, technological marvels capable of delivering more airpower to distant places more rapidly than any ships in history.

They were the most powerful ships America's naval engi-neers and architects had ever produced, built to fight a war that had not yet begun.

In July 1940, the Navy ordered three *Essex*-class carriers from Newport News and Shipbuilding. The ships of this class were to be named in honor of historic vessels and Revolu-tionary War battles. CV-9 was the *Essex*. CV-10 initially was to be the *Bonhomme Richard* but was renamed *Yorktown* after the original *Yorktown* was sunk by Japanese bombers and torpedo planes in June 1942's Battle of Midway.

CV-11 became the USS *Intrepid*.

Surprisingly, there is no general consensus why aircraft car-riers are identified by the code CV. The *C*, it is believed, means *cruiser class*; although the Navy's first carrier, the *Langley*, was a converted collier, it was believed that carriers would eventu-ally replace cruisers. But the derivation of the *V* remains ques-tionable: in 1920, while blimps and dirigibles were identified by *Z* for *zeppelin* after their German inventor, the Navy desig-nated heavier-than-air craft V, perhaps coming from the French word *volplane*, basically meaning a machine held in the air by wings. The V signified a vessel designed for aviation. Thus CV: a cruiser capable of recovering and launching airplanes. The number 11 designates *Intrepid* as the 11th Essex class carrier.

Intrepid's keel, the ship's spine, was laid down at Newport News on December 1, 1941. Construction was completed in an astonishing 15 months—almost a year and a half earlier than the originally scheduled launch. *Intrepid* was desperately needed. In one respect, America had been incredibly fortunate on December 7, 1941; when the Japanese launched the surprise attack on Pearl Harbor, not a single aircraft carrier had been caught in port. That was a matter of luck rather than strategy. Battleship Row was devastated. Four of those mighty warships had been sunk. Four others were severely damaged. But the Navy's carrier fleet had survived completely intact— and the outcome of the war would turn on that.

The stunning success of the attack on Pearl Harbor by warplanes from six Japanese carriers had instantly revolutionized naval warfare. The ability of hundreds of airplanes to appear out of the mists to strike a target thousands of miles from Japan had shocked the Western nations. Battleships no longer ruled the oceans.

Throughout 1942, control of the Pacific Ocean and the fate of East Asia depended on the ability of a few, mostly aging American carriers to stop Japanese expansion. In April, only four months after that day of infamy, Colonel Jimmy Doolittle's 16 lumbering B-25s thrilled the wounded nation by taking off from the *Hornet* and successfully dropping bombs on Tokyo. A month later, in the first naval battle ever fought in which the ships never were in sight of the enemy, carrier planes in the Coral Sea hunted down and devastated the Japanese warships. In June, Japanese expansion had been stopped at Midway. By August, carriers were supporting Marine landings at Guadalcanal.

The cost had been high: in May, *Lexington* had been torpedoed and sunk and *Yorktown* badly damaged in the Battle of the Coral Sea. A month later, the hastily repaired *Yorktown* was sunk at Midway. In August, *Enterprise* took three direct hits and several near misses, suffering heavy damage during the Battle of the Eastern Solomons. The first week of September, *Saratoga*, which initially had been designed as a battlecruiser but was converted into one of the Navy's first aircraft carriers in 1928, was torpedoed off the Solomons and had to be towed back to Pearl Harbor. Weeks later, *Wasp* was torpedoed and sunk southeast of San Cristobal Island. In late October, *Hornet*, hit by dive-bombers and aerial torpedoes during the Battle of Santa Cruz, went down.

By late 1942, the Navy did not have a single undamaged aircraft carrier in the Pacific.

The situation was only slightly better in the Atlantic. Ironically, literally minutes before *Intrepid* was christened, German radio claimed that U-boat *404* had torpedoed and sunk the *Ranger*, the first American ship designed and built as an aircraft carrier, in the North Atlantic.

The *Essex*-class carriers were desperately needed. As Vice Admiral John McCain told reporters, "Naval aviation has become an extremely powerful weapon, possibly the most powerful . . . Huge task forces, spearheaded by carrier-based aircraft, are poising the new pile driver blows against the enemy . . ." [Preparing to] "smash the enemy into complete defeat."

Intrepid about to be christened at the Newport News Shipbuilding and Dry Dock Company, April 26, 1943. *Collection of the Intrepid Museum. Gift of Mrs. William H. Hoover. P2009.13.03*

The first of the new class, appropriately named *Essex*, was launched in July 1942. The new *Yorktown* was launched in January 1943, *Intrepid* three months later. The invited guests at *Intrepid*'s commissioning included Vice Admiral Hoover, who had commanded both the *Langley* and *Lexington*; his daughter Jeanne Hoover, who served as her mother's maid of honor; Supervisor of Construction at Newport News Rear Admiral O.I. Cox; Rear Admiral Van Keuren, director of the Naval Research Laboratory, then secretly at work on the atom bomb; Captain Russell Crenshaw, assistant commandant of the 5th Naval District; Captain Webster M. Thompson, production officer of the Norfolk Navy Yard; and local yard officials.

But no one watched the ceremony with more interest or excitement than Captain Thomas Lamison Sprague, who only days earlier had been appointed CFO, connection fitting-out officer, of the USS *Intrepid*. It would be his job to give this miracle of engineering its soul. He would welcome the crew and airplanes aboard, he would find the deficiencies and weaknesses and correct them, he would put it to sea and fire its guns, he would launch its planes, and eventually he would command it in combat.

Tom Sprague had spent his life preparing for this job. It was only a week after he'd celebrated his ninth birthday that Professor Langley's Buzzard dropped into the Potomac. Two months later, the Wright brothers conquered gravity.

It was an amazing time to be young in America. The impossible was becoming reality. A year before Sprague was born in 1894, the Duryea brothers had produced the first American "motocycle," as the horseless carriage initially was called. He was still in elementary school in Lima, Ohio, when the Wright boys, whose five cycle shops were just about 70 miles down the road in Dayton, had proved controlled, manned flight was possible.

Tom Sprague had witnessed the birth and growth of American naval aviation—and he had even played a small role in its growth. Flying had become his passion. He wanted to fly, he intended to fly, he was going to fly—whatever it took. After graduating from Annapolis, class of 1917, he began applying to the new flight school. Unfortunately, a lot of Navy commanders considered flight training a waste of vital resources. To them, "naval aviation" was a contradiction in terms. Navy meant ships, not airplanes. The word itself, *navy*, was derived from the Latin word *navis*, meaning "pertaining to ships." In fact, in 1919, Chief of Naval Operations Admiral William Benson had attempted to close down the Navy's aeronautics program, saying he could not "conceive of any use the fleet will ever have for aviation." His decision was reversed by Assistant Secretary of the Navy Franklin Delano Roosevelt, who believed Navy planes might someday prove useful.

Even so, it was generally accepted that the Navy needed fine young officers like Tom Sprague on the bridge—not in a cockpit. During his first sea duty as gun division officer on the *Cleveland,* his commanding officer wrote that he "Gives promise of developing into an excellent officer . . . [although] He still has much to learn." And his commander aboard the armored cruiser USS *Brooklyn,* for example, refused to endorse his request to attend flight school because "at the present time there is no competent Engineer Officer available in this force as a relief for Lieutenant Sprague."

Sprague persisted. "I have always requested aviation duty on fitness reports, etc.," Sprague wrote to the Navy's Department of Personnel. He had to apply three times before his request for flight training was finally approved.

He entered flight school at the Aviation Training School, Pensacola, in November 1920, earning his wings as a naval aviator 10 months later. He had learned to fly on a Curtiss N9—a seaplane with a maximum speed of 78 mph—because the Navy had not yet embraced the potential of aircraft carriers. Few people believed it was feasible for an airplane to land on the rocking deck of a ship at sea. Instead, it was predicted hydroplanes would take off from cruisers, scout for the enemy fleet, then land alongside their ship to be lifted aboard by crane.

But there were some officers who believed planes might play a larger role in the service. In July 1921, just as Sprague was finishing flight school, Army General Billy Mitchell stunned military experts by proving that great warships could be sunk by bombers, a feat they did not believe possible. In a controlled demonstration, his planes destroyed a submarine, a destroyer, a cruiser, and a battleship—the *Ostfriesland*, which had been surrendered by Germany at the end of the Great War. Although the anchored, defenseless ships were little more than floating targets, newspapers reported that "some admirals sobbed like babies" when the *Ostfriesland* went down. In those few days, Billy Mitchell's Martin MB-2 bombers had established both the capability and the necessity of a naval air force, reminding military leaders, "1,000 bombardment airplanes can be built and operated for about the price of one battleship."

And a small number of those planes could sink a mighty dreadnought. This demonstration, which many military officials derided and dismissed as "rigged," also sank the Navy's future plans. Leading members of Congress, rather than funding the construction of new battleships, instead dismissed them as "obsolete" and urged the service to add additional "airplane tenders" to the fleet.

Tom Sprague and his classmates had graduated into the rapidly evolving Navy, which was reluctantly accepting the potential power of naval aviation. These young flyboys, scarves trailing from their open cockpits, would shape the future.

After spending almost a year on the staff of the Commander Aircraft Squadrons, Battle Force for the Pacific Fleet, as the Navy tried to figure out the most effective means of utilizing airplanes, Sprague received his first assignment at sea as an aviator aboard the aircraft tender *Aroostook*. A converted minelayer, *Aroostook* carried floatplanes to be used for observation.

Everything about Navy aviation was new and mostly untested. It was a time rife with opportunities for a man to prove his mettle, a perfect time for men like Tom Sprague. He was a tinkerer. He enjoyed wrestling with intriguing tactical problems and took pride in finding solutions. That was one of the things he admired most about the Wright brothers. Among the most serious problems facing naval aviators at that time was how to communicate effectively—and from long distances—with their ships. Two-way communications between ground stations and planes was brand-new, and increasing the range and quality of plane-to-ship communications became Tom Sprague's goal. As *Aroostook*'s Captain H.V. Butler noted, "The performance of his duties has been excellent. He has made a study of aircraft radio and his knowledge and ability has done a great deal to increase the efficiency of aircraft radio in the organization."

It's impossible to know if Sprague considered himself a sailor who flew or a pilot who sailed. In 1926, following a three-year stint as a test pilot and instructor at Pensacola, he was assigned to the fabled USS *Langley*. CV-1, as it was known officially, had been recommissioned as an aircraft carrier four years earlier—its large coal storage hold converted into a place to park planes—to serve as a floating laboratory, a place to test theories and conduct aviation experiments in search of the elusive horizon, that place where warships and flying machines came together to create the most formidable weapon in history.

Langley was a makeshift platform, a deck laid on top of a coal carrier. Its crew referred to it as the Covered Wagon, but more often it was referred to derisively as "this poor comic ship." But it worked. It proved planes could take off from its deck and land. And in fact, several of the elements in the original design—an open hangar deck, for example—became standard on purpose-built carriers.

Sprague had risen steadily through the ranks, still tinkering, pioneering new and better ways of flying higher and safer—and completing the mission. In 1928, while serving as senior aviation officer on the battleship *Maryland*, "Lieutenant Sprague invented . . . and manufactured means for accurately determining the bearing of an unseen target." While testing his invention, he managed to overcome "motor trouble, succeeding in increasing the revolutions of his motor which permitted him to remain in the air," although eventually he was forced to land "lacking gas, oil and water." Commander J.V. Kleeman noted that this young officer, who was "clearly superior in every category," had only one defect. He lacked "patience."

In 1933, while commanding the air wing of a cruiser squadron, now Lieutenant Commander Sprague received a commendation from the fleet commander for his work "in the science of aerial navigation at sea" that provided "a distinct advance . . . that can easily and accurately be used in the confined space available in an airplane."

In assignments on land, at sea, or in the air, Sprague received the highest grades on his duty fitness reports. The real question was where he fit best, how to use his talents. In 1933 he was appointed Superintendent of the Navy's Aeronautical

Engine Laboratory at the Philadelphia Navy Yard, where he was praised for his "very broad and comprehensive knowledge of aeronautics, as well as varied practical experience in aviation. He has shown especial aptitude in supervision of the Aeronautical Engine Laboratory . . . possessing a broad knowledge of aeronautics and internal combustion engines."

He then spent a year as *Saratoga's* air officer, for which he was lauded by Captain W.F. "Bull" Halsey—a daring carrier officer who would be a leader of the Pacific fleet—as "especially intelligent, alert, enthusiastic, loyal and cooperative. An officer of the highest personal and military principles."

He was proving to be equally adept in the air and on the ocean, returning to the *Langley* as navigator, then back to Pensacola for three years to run the entire aviation training program. In June 1940, he was assigned to USS *Ranger* as its executive officer, commanding its air operations. During his year in that post, "some 4,000 landings have been made . . . under all kinds of operating conditions, none of which have resulted in casualties to material or personnel."

While aboard *Ranger*, he received special recognition for his performance "operating under the trying conditions of the limited emergency." It was a casual mention from Captain A.E. Montgomery, typed at the bottom of a performance report. The details of this emergency were not included, just the observation that this officer performed well under pressure, but it would prove to be prescient three years later when Sprague faced the most difficult challenge of his Navy life.

Military careers quite often are determined by chance. The reaction to opportunity creates heroes. Men and women who rise to the challenge are rewarded. Sprague had traveled around the world chasing action, but on December 7, 1941, he was in command of the seaplane tender USS *Pocomoke* far from the eye of the storm. *Pocomoke*, named for a sound in Maryland where an Indian tribe of that name once lived, was operating off the coast of Argentia, Newfoundland. Sprague had taken command of the ship during the summer, supervising its conversion from the cargo ship SS *Exchequer*, notable as the first all-welded steel ship hull, into a Navy vessel. It was a necessary but tedious job. German wolf packs were on the prowl in the North Atlantic, relentlessly attacking convoys delivering desperately needed supplies to England. Sprague supervised the flight operations of two seaplanes protecting those convoys from the U-boats.

So while the world caught fire, while the Navy was fighting for survival in the Pacific, Sprague seemed stuck across the American continent, far away from the smoldering ruins of the fleet in Pearl Harbor. He gritted his teeth, read the newspapers, and did his assigned job—but never stopped reaching out to the brass for a combat assignment. He wrote letters and made phone calls, he spoke with friends and acquaintances, doing anything and everything possible to get into the war.

The Navy had other plans for him. In February, he assumed command of USS *Charger*, supervising its conversion from a passenger/cargo ship built to sail the east coast of South America into an escort carrier. After completing the conversion "with marked energy and efficiency," as Rear Admiral A.D. Bernhard reported, Sprague took *Charger* into Chesapeake Bay, where it trained carrier pilots and crews.

From his first fitness reports two decades earlier, he had been requesting assignment to "a carrier" in the "battle fleet."

But to his frustration, Sprague had gained a reputation for his expertise in preparing ships, planes, and men for action. The Navy needed carrier pilots. It needed plane handlers and landing signal officers and firemen and ordinance loaders and mechanics, and all the myriad skills required for a carrier to function—and Sprague was an acknowledged master of training, motivation, and machinery.

His success in that command was noted: Admiral Ernest McWhorter reported Sprague was "an exceptionally able officer and best fitted to command a new large carrier." Admiral Arthur Davis, who helped develop dive-bombing techniques for carrier-based planes, wrote, "I consider him one of the best qualified officers in the service for major aircraft carrier command."

Few officers had been better trained or were more qualified than Tom Sprague to assume command of a carrier. The brass knew that. By regulation, in fact, only naval aviators could command a carrier. The problem was, there were too few carriers in the fleet. But new boats were coming. The shipyards were performing mechanical miracles, completing construction that normally took years in months and repairs that might have required months in weeks.

Sprague—and the rapidly growing number of Navy-trained pilots—had watched with fascination and, undoubtedly, trepidation as battleship purists had fought the champions of aircraft carriers for strategic supremacy—and Congressional dollars. Although the Navy was building a carrier fleet before Pearl Harbor, many politicians and military officials still considered carriers little more than overly expensive and highly vulnerable toys, questioning how they might be strategically deployed in naval warfare. Until the first shots were fired, no one could know for certain how valuable they might be. "Carriers are like two blindfolded men armed with daggers in a ring," Admiral Henry Butler had noted in 1930, "there is apt to be sudden destruction to one or both of them."

The German military tended to agree. Hitler's high command, for example, decided to focus on a land-based Luftwaffe capable of reaching anyplace in Europe, believing that its technically advanced planes and powerful shore guns could prevent any attack from the sea. Against the wishes of Air Marshal Hermann Goering, the Nazis' Kriegsmarine initially planned to build four carriers. Goering did everything possible to scuttle the project, and his brilliant aviation designers never created a carrier-based plane capable of fighting Allied air forces. The Nazis' only carrier, KMS *Graf Zeppelin*, eventually was 80% completed before construction was halted in 1943.

Meanwhile, the British Royal Navy attempted to create a hybrid vessel, a powerful battlewagon able to launch and recover ships, but it was eventually considered impractical and abandoned.

Gradually, especially as bombers able to carry more potent weapons longer distances were developed, military leaders finally embraced the reality of fast, floating airfields. Beginning with the Naval Expansion Act of 1938, 32 *Essex*-class carriers were approved. Eventually 24 of them would be commissioned. *Intrepid* was third.

And it would be sailed into the war by Captain Thomas Sprague.

The call he had been working for finally came from Fleet
Admiral Ernest J. King in April 1943. Admiral King made
the decision on all major combat assignments. The initial rec-
ommendation had been made by the Bureau of Naval Personnel, but it was Ernest King who moved his officers across
the oceans like chess pieces. He knew his people; most of the
Navy leaders came from a relatively small group of Annapolis
grads who had been crossing paths on various ships and shore
assignments for decades between the wars. Many of them had
come up through the ranks together, leaving behind those
who could not keep up in their wake.

As a pilot and the former head of the Navy's Bureau of
Aeronautics, King knew Tom Sprague well. Having grown up
in Lorin, Ohio, about 140 miles from Sprague's hometown,
he also knew they shared the same Midwestern upbringing—
although King had a reputation as a hands-on ladies' man, while
Sprague was happily married and had two children. What the
two men had in common, though, was a reputation for being
whip-smart, dependable and resilient and tough enough to meet
the most difficult challenges. King was so tough, it was said,
he shaved with a blowtorch. And that was the type of man he
wanted in command of his ships.

Sprague had earned this command, and King was pleased
to appoint him to it. As he liked to do, he had called Sprague
personally to deliver the news. It was not a surprise. Ever
since Sprague was temporarily promoted to rear admiral in
December 1943, the scuttlebutt had been that Tom Sprague
was going to get *Intrepid*.

He was in his office at Quonset Point, Rhode Island,
working as chief of staff for Rear Admiral Pat Bellinger,

commander of the Atlantic Fleet's Aviation Division, when King reached him. As soon as Sprague heard an ensign tell him, "Hold for Admiral King, please," he knew it was true.

"Tom? Ernie King here."

"Good to hear from you, Admiral." Sprague's heart was playing a Sousa march. This was a call that would change his life.

"I'm calling to tell you we're giving you *Intrepid*. Congratulations! You've earned it." Orders to follow.

On April 11, 1943, Captain Thomas Sprague reported to Newport News for his new duty, "involving flying in connection with the fitting out of the USS *Intrepid* . . . and for duty involving flying as commanding officer of that vessel when placed in commission."

Two weeks later, Tom and Evelyn Sprague were sitting on the platform erected for *Intrepid*'s christening ceremony. As he listened to the speeches drone on, it was impossible not to look back on his career. The Navy had taken a raw kid from small-town Ohio and educated him, trained him, shaped him, and prepared him to command this great ship.

While Chaplain Neyman concluded his remarks, Tom Sprague stared at the podium and squeezed his wife Evelyn's hand. She had earned this moment too.

They had been married 23 years ago, in a small ceremony in her parents' home in San Diego. Evelyn Curry had worn her grandmother's white satin gown with a lace overdress. She was a fine match for the dashing young lieutenant, having been educated in England and France and serving in the Women's Motor Corps—using her own car—during the Great War. He admired everything about her. He used to brag to friends that she could knit a scarf and keep track of a baseball game on the radio while taking part in a conversation about world events. Although, he admitted somewhat ruefully, she couldn't boil water without burning it!

She had stood with him through all his many ships and assignments, sharing all the victories and disappointments as he rose through the ranks. She was the ultimate military wife; it was Evelyn who had raised their children while he was at sea, Evelyn who had been there in 1933 when their 6-year-old son, Tom Jr., had suddenly taken ill and died. It was Evelyn who had diligently packed up their homes each time they moved to his next duty station. They had been through so many beginnings together. This was still another one. Evelyn knew exactly the meaning of that gentle squeeze: *it's our time*. Finally.

During his career, Sprague had served on eight different ships, among them the aircraft carriers *Langley*, *Saratoga*, and *Ranger*, but those ships had been built in the 1920s and early '30s, and none of them rivaled this modern, massive, beautiful ship.

Every moment of his career had been built into this ship. He and his contemporaries, the men with whom he had flown or trained or supervised, had helped build it just as much as if they had hammered down the planks of its wooden deck. The lessons they had learned from every one of tens of thousands of takeoffs and landings on beautiful sunny days in calm seas or dark turbulent nights when the sea was screaming had been incorporated into its design and construction to make it the most lethal weapon ever produced. It was designed to strike the enemy wherever he was and then come home safely.

Men would die on this ship. Sprague knew that. Looking at it floating calmly, so pristine, so perfect, it was hard to imagine the horrors that lay in its future. Pilots would take off and never return, the gun batteries would be tested, the Japanese would be relentless. It was a floating fortress. Every effort had been made to protect its crew, but that couldn't change the reality of combat: *Intrepid* would be bloodied under his command.

The Navy was putting 3,000 men, a hundred or more airplanes, and this mammoth ship in his hands. The burden of command, as it is sometimes described, is an awesome responsibility. He was going to be accountable for every aspect of *Intrepid*'s operations, its personnel and its mission, its safety and security, its success or failure. He was going to be forced to make instant, critical decisions under in combat, life-and-death decisions, often with incomplete information. He had been training for all this since those first days as a plebe at Annapolis, when he barely knew port from starboard and wandered aimlessly trying to find the head.

At that moment, it was impossible not to recall those flimsy biplanes that bumped along the winds, those days he had watched the ocean come dangerously close to his open cockpit, the debates about carriers, his first landing at sea, the brief terror of being lost in the night skies and unable to find the *Saratoga*, the thrill of settling into new and more powerful airplanes, the small technological advances that one by one by one had led to this day, this ship, this *Intrepid*.

The *Essex*-class carriers were the result of all the lessons that had been learned since Eugene Ely had flown his Model

D off *Birmingham*. *Intrepid* was designed and constructed to be the most powerful warship in history. Built at a cost of $44 million, the ship was 87 feet long and 93 feet 2 inches wide at the waterline, while its flight deck was 147 feet 6 inches wide, dimensions that allowed it to just barely pass through the Panama Canal into the Pacific Ocean. It displaced 36,000 tons fully loaded and was capable of racing through the oceans at 33 knots—more than twice the speed of the *Langley*. It was capable of carrying 6,000 tons of fuel, enough to cruise 10,700 miles at 25 knots and more than 17,000 miles at 15 knots—more than halfway around the world.

She was powered by eight Babcock & Wilcox steam boilers, which generated steam at 850°F of pressure at 565 pounds per square inch, more than enough for its four Westinghouse turbines to turn four propeller shafts—generating an incredible 150,000 horsepower. Steering was controlled by a single massive 430-square-foot rudder, a stainless steel shaft larger than a handball court wall. It was among the largest rudders ever put on a ship.

Essex-class carriers also were better armed and armored than the earlier classes. While its air group made it a devastating offensive weapon its anti-aircraft defense included 151 guns; an array of 20mm Oerlikon cannons, 40mm Bofors guns, and 5"/38 cal. weapons.

Intrepid had been designed to carry more airpower than the *Yorktown*-class carriers. It was 60 feet longer and 10 feet wider than those ships. Its larger flight deck enabled it to carry 100 or more warplanes, plus spare parts. Among them were a mix of Grumman F6F Hellcats, Douglas Dauntless dive-bombers, and torpedo-dropping Grumman Avengers. A deck-edge elevator on the hangar deck, made it capable of launching more planes more quickly and efficiently than its predecessors.

And unlike British or Japanese flattops, the hangar deck, where planes were stored and repaired, was larger and open-ended, allowing the Essex-class to carry considerably more planes than any carrier ever built. Also, while the Brits chose the added protection of an armored flight deck, the US and Japan armored only that lower hangar deck. The enclosed hangar deck adopted by the Royal Navy, as well as the Imperial Japanese Navy, provided added protection during attacks, but the lack of ventilation prohibited engines from being warmed up before being raised to the flight deck.

The trade-off was simple and controversial: crew safety versus launch time. *Essex*-class carriers were designed to launch more aircraft more quickly than any carrier in history. As a result, *Intrepid* had an open hangar deck—it even had an impressive hangar deck catapult enabling crews to launch planes from there.

Eventually, that choice would require an extraordinarily innovative—and historic—solution to save *Intrepid*.

Tom Sprague knew her every inch, from the nuts and the bolts to the number of replacement parts stored below. He knew the miles of electric wiring and the intricacies of a secret radar system he had helped develop; he knew which watertight doors had to be closed to seal each numbered compartment. He knew the sound of the engines humming at full speed, the roar of a flight deck in action, the food that the mess would serve her 3,000-man company and the thunder of the guns that would protect them.

And he knew where the body bags were stored.

On that beautiful April day, *Intrepid* was as perfect as a dream, untouched by the reality of war. But as Tom Sprague knew, that was about to change.

TWO

ON MONDAY MORNING, December 8, 1941, while the nation was reeling from the Japanese surprise attack, newspapers around the country innocently published a previously circulated Associated Press story entitled "U.S. Boasts Naval Fortress at Pearl Harbor in Hawaii." The article had been intended to reinforce the confidence Americans had in the nation's military strength and preparedness. "The Hawaiian Islands stand at the crossroads of the Pacific," it read, "approximately one-third of the way across the vast ocean separating the United States and Japan.

"In these islands the United States has constructed a great naval fortress, centered in the naval base and dry dock at Pearl Harbor on the picturesque Island of Oahu. This harbor, 60 feet deep and some 10 square miles in area, can accommodate the entire U.S. Fleet . . . The strategic location of Hawaii and the great defense works centered there make the territory a major key to war in the Far East."

The fact that this puff piece appeared only hours after the most devastating attack on American territory in history instead revealed how completely unprepared the nation was for war with Japan.

While the American military had predicted the Japanese would attack somewhere sometime—the Navy had even conducted surprise attack exercises at Pearl Harbor—the scope and success of the attack were far greater than anyone had believed possible.

In the chaos during and immediately following the attack, President Franklin Roosevelt received only partial and sometimes inaccurate reports. Supposedly, for example, he was told "two of the Japanese planes [attacking Pearl Harbor] were known to have a swastika on them," and that the simultaneous attack on the Philippine Islands that took place that day had been followed hours later by an additional strike on Manila.

In Washington, long before the full scale of the devastation was known, while the fight to save lives and ships still was raging at Pearl Harbor, Roosevelt met in his White House study with military and diplomatic leaders. Among the first to arrive was Secretary of the Navy Frank Knox. During this and subsequent meetings, it became apparent that the military had no strategy to deal with this situation. Experts had spent the two decades since the end of the Great War preparing a response for every type of attack imaginable, but every one of those scenarios required the use of a powerful fleet of battleships—a fleet that no longer existed.

The most realistic plan came from Admiral King, who had said bluntly, "Hold what you've got and hit them where you can."

There was only one small bit of optimism in the reports Roosevelt received: "There are two task forces at sea. Each of them with a carrier." In fact, while the attack had put the nation's battlewagons out of action, at least temporarily, the

Navy had seven aircraft carriers of varying sizes and resources available. While potentially they were a fearsome force, in reality, they were untested in combat. No one knew what they were capable of accomplishing. But through the first few months of World War II, America would have to rely on them to "hold what you've got."

The battle for control of the Pacific began on February 1, 1942, less than two months after Pearl Harbor, when two carrier task forces led by *Yorktown* and *Enterprise* attacked the Japanese garrisons on the Marshall and Gilbert Islands. The raid destroyed 38 Japanese planes and damaged nine ships, several runways, and fuel depots. While it had little military impact, it greatly boosted morale: "Navy Blasts Enemy's Pacific Bases" headlined the *Nashville Tennessean*. The *Honolulu Advertiser* reported, "Many Enemy Planes, Ships Are Destroyed." "Fleet's Power Unleashed Again" wrote the *Honolulu Star-Bulletin*, adding, "Senator John Overton of Louisiana told the Senate today that the United States Pacific fleet attack against the Marshall and Gilbert Islands is only 'the opening gun of the American navy in the great battle in which we are now engaged.'"

Carriers had passed their first tentative test; they had struck the enemy on his territory. Important lessons had been learned. For the first time, hundreds of bombers were armed, launched, and successfully recovered under combat conditions.

Every day brought new challenges. On February 20, Japanese bombers from the island of Bougainville attacked the *Lexington*. Their approach was detected by rudimentary radar, and 16 of 18 bombers were shot down. In that fighting, Lieutenant Commander Edward "Butch" O'Hare, who had earned his wings at Pensacola under Superintendent of

Aviation Training Tom Sprague, shot down five enemy planes, becoming the first naval aviator in the war to earn the Congressional Medal of Honor.

Shattering the Japanese belief that spreading its troops on numerous islands throughout the Pacific provided greater security than massing larger forces on a few heavily fortified bases, in March, 100 bombers from *Lexington* and *Yorktown* surprised defenders on New Guinea by attacking from the far side of the island, coming in low over jungles and mountains and sinking five warships and five transports and damaging four other ships.

A month later, Jimmy Doolittle proved carrier-based planes could reach the heart of the Japanese empire when his 16 B-25Bs launched from the *Hornet*—incredibly using only 450 feet to take off compared to the usual 1,200 feet—and bombed Tokyo, Kobe, Nagoya, and Yokohama.

In May, the first carrier battle in history took place in the Coral Sea. During five days of combat, as wave after wave of American and Japanese planes relentlessly attacked, the warships remained more than 200 miles apart, never sighting the enemy.

During the fighting, *Yorktown* took a direct hit but was able to repair the severe damage. *Lexington* survived being bombed and torpedoed, remaining afloat for several hours as its crew successfully fought fires. It wasn't enough; gasoline vapors trapped deep belowdecks ignited and exploded, forcing the task force to scuttle the Lady Lex. But the Japanese also suffered significant losses—and abandoned their effort to occupy Port Moresby. For the first time, Japanese expansion had been stopped.

Any lingering doubts about the vital role carriers would play in the war ended forever the first week of June. American intelligence had broken Japanese codes, which revealed that a massive invasion force, led by four carriers and several battleships, was speeding toward Midway Island. Two American task forces, including three carriers, raced to meet them. On June 4, Admiral Chester Nimitz warned the American fleet and the garrison on Midway that the rapidly approaching Japanese fleet was only 500 miles away. The enemy fleet was an extraordinary target. Unlike American naval strategy, in which numerous smaller carrier groups sailing independently would come together when necessary to create a larger force, Japanese carriers sailed in a massive formation known as Kidō Butai, meaning "a mobile force," with as many as six carriers and more than 400 planes capable of overwhelming most targets it encountered.

But it also made them extremely vulnerable.

That morning, dive-bombers, torpedo planes, and fighters from *Enterprise* and *Yorktown* flew out of the rising sun and destroyed three enemy carriers: *Kaga*, *Akagi*, and *Soryu*. Later that day, squadrons from *Hornet* and *Enterprise* damaged the *Hiryu* so severely it had to be scuttled.

Each of these Japanese carriers had participated in the attack on Pearl Harbor. Payback had begun.

Midway was a huge defeat for Japan. Four carriers were lost, three battleships and two cruisers were badly damaged, an estimated 275 planes were shot down or sunk with the carriers and more than 3,000 sailors and pilots were killed or wounded. Many of them were veteran pilots who could not easily be replaced. The losses at Midway halted the Japanese offensive.

American losses were small compared to the enemy's. During four days of fighting, only the *Yorktown* had been sunk, 150 planes were lost, and about 300 men had been killed.

For the Japanese, replacing those lost carriers was far more difficult than for America. By this time, for example, *Intrepid* was off the drawing board and already far ahead of its construction schedule. After being christened in April, a precommissioning crew began conducting basic sea trials to ensure that the ship met Navy standards and that all its equipment—from mess ovens to every one of its 151 guns and cannon—were working properly.

These crew members were proud "black shoes," the men who would keep the ship functioning, as opposed to the "brown shoes," the naval aviators who would eventually come aboard and carry the fight to the enemy. Pilots had begun wearing those brown shoes in 1913, supposedly to hide the dirt from airfields, but also serving to distinguish them from the sailors whose shoes traditionally were black from tar and coal dust.

Among the men who joined the crew during those first days were Lieutenant Commander Phil Reynolds, Chief Boatswain's Mate Frank Johnson, and Chief Warrant Officer Richard Montfort. Both Reynolds and Johnson were career Navy, having enlisted in the summer of 1919, but had followed very different paths; 18-year-old Reynolds began his career that June as an Annapolis midshipman, while in August, 19-year-old Johnson signed his papers at the recruiting station in his hometown of Portsmouth, New Hampshire, and became an ordinary seaman.

Phil Reynolds came aboard as first lieutenant and the ship's damage control officer. It was a key role. Every carrier that saw combat suffered substantial damage. In several cases, the ship—and the lives of its crew—had been saved by the split-second decisions of its damage control officer. And, months later, the fate of the *Intrepid* would depend on him.

Reynolds was large, good-natured bulldog of a man with a full head of hair parted almost in the middle and a carefully cultivated mustache. At the academy, his classmates noted his large ears "that would protect him from the elements," and throughout his career, he had fought an occasionally losing battle to keep his weight under control. While serving as watch and division officer on the battleship *Utah* in 1934, for example, it was noted he "appears overweight."

In some ways, he bore a vague resemblance to burly Academy Award–winning movie star Wallace Beery, then among the highest paid actors in the world. And like Beery, he was capable of performing a great variety of roles. But Phil Reynolds's girth never stopped him from squeezing into every area on the brand-new *Intrepid*.

The native of Ventura, California, was a detail man. His job required him not just to know all areas of the ship, but also to understand how they functioned, how they worked in harmony with other machinery and, in an extreme case, how they could quickly be repaired when damaged or replaced if lost. During the fitting-out period, he would roam the ship, studying blueprints, learning every system the way Rockefellers knew oil wells.

Unlike many of his Annapolis classmates, upon graduation Reynolds had rejected an opportunity to fly. "Family objections," he explained. Although "Personally, I would like aviation duty . . . I have promised not to request aviation duty." What he did want, he wrote over and over, was assignment to "a battleship" or just "a combatant ship" where he might have "gunnery or engineering duty . . . to round out my experience."

Phil Reynold's career was proof that the popular phrase "join the Navy and see the world" was entirely accurate. In 1924, Ensign Reynolds reported to the destroyer USS *Pruitt*, which had been part of the force dispatched to China after the provisional president of China, Sun Yat-Sen, threatened American business interests. Fighting had broken out among various Chinese factions, and heavily armed sailors frequently were sent ashore to protect American citizens and property. Reynolds led several landing parties. While he spoke only a smattering of Chinese, his threatening scowl successfully communicated his intent: if necessary, he would shoot.

Reynolds spent most of the first three years of his career in the Far East, earning the Navy Expeditionary Medal with a bronze star, awarded to men "who engaged in operations against armed opposition or operated under circumstances . . . deemed to merit special recognition."

He did get that gunnery experience he requested when assigned to the aging battleship *Utah* in 1930, although not in the way he expected. Reynolds liked to tell people that he was "the first officer assigned to turret two during bombing practices after *Utah* was converted into a mobile target. Turret was struck by 14 bombs while I was in it." That made him, he bragged, "the leading bomb-catcher in the entire United States Navy."

Following that, he had a variety of assignments both on ships and ashore. He was, wrote *Utah* Captain Frederick, "A fine officer who will take any job given to him and get results." In 1933, for example, he was commended for his work helping to maintain order and assisting in rescue work when a massive earthquake struck Long Beach, California, where 150 people were killed and as many as 1,000 more were injured. His calm demeanor amidst a crisis was exemplary, and with his team, he "did much to relieve the distress and suffering, as well as in preventing further death, injury or loss of property."

And while serving on the great battleship USS *Arizona* in 1939 as watch and division officer, his secondary duties included "Sailing and Rowing officer."

Reynolds was a man of many esoteric talents; he spoke un peu *français*, played a questionable clarinet in the Naval Academy orchestra, and owned a coffee plantation in Costa Rica with his brother, who managed it. At Annapolis, he joined the literary societies and was known to be a good fellow; as his classmates described him in their yearbook, *Lucky Bag*, "At present remains a true friend of dogs—girls being only side issues. (Thus the dogs gain!)"

Phil Reynolds was one of those affable men whose friendly attitude belied his steel spine. No one crossed him twice. When a situation needed resolution, whether Chinese warlords were threatening violence or a ship was losing power in a storm, he was a man you wanted at your side. Like Sprague, he wanted to be in the middle of the action. Although he had served on three battleships—*Arizona*, *Utah*, and *Colorado*—he repeatedly requested assignment to "A battleship on the west coast," or "Any destroyer in the Battle Fleet," and, failing that, "Any heavy cruiser attached to the Scouting Force" or any "Combatant ship with home port in . . . San Diego," where his wife and son lived.

When the Japanese attacked, he was in command of an aging minesweeper, the USS *Cormorant*—which was resting quietly in dry dock in Puget Sound. Contrary to his wish list—he wanted to get into the action—in March 1942 he was ordered to Annapolis, where he taught marine engineering, forced to watch the war from the safety of a college campus.

In all its brutality, combat is seductive. It remains the ultimate test of character; Reynolds had stood tall against warlords and local bandits in China, but the greatest war in history was passing him by. He desperately wanted to be there, to see it, to experience it. He had spent two decades training for it. He was ready. Ready? More than ready. He continued to apply for duty at sea.

In May 1943, he finally got his chance, joining Tom Sprague to take the sparkling new *Intrepid* through its final fitting out and shakedown cruise. And then, if everything went right, he would go to war.

Sprague greeted him on the bridge. They exchanged salutes and shook hands. "Welcome aboard," Sprague said.

"Happy to be with you, sir."

Sprague poured him a welcoming cup of coffee as he gave a rough overview of the shaping-up schedule. There was a tremendous amount of work to be done before the ship was ready to join the fleet. While the two men had never met, they knew each other in the way Navy vets shared a common experience. They reached back into their careers, as long ago as the academy, to find people and places they both knew. They shared memories and found places to come together. In this way, they began to build the bond, the trust that would become absolutely essential to prepare the ship, train its crew, and take it into combat.

They sat there through the morning, getting on the same page. As Reynolds finally prepared to take his first tour of his new ship, Sprague asked, "You ready?"

Reynolds laughed at that. "Been ready for the last decade."

Phil Reynolds had applied to Annapolis intending to make the Navy his career, but for Frank Elbridge Johnson, the Navy basically offered a good job. In 1917, as the war in Europe was spreading, Congress increased the size of the Navy to 87,000 men. To fill those new slots, the service mounted a nationwide advertising campaign: "Help your country and help yourself by enlisting in the Navy, the first line of defense," read one poster. "It offers active service at the start; no long periods of training camps or barracks. After two months you are on a ship and in the thick of it. Pay is good and all clear money, actual expenses low. Every man gets a fair deal and, for good men, promotion is rapid."

Johnson was one of tens of thousands of young men who took that fair deal. In almost every way, he was the opposite of the physically imposing Reynolds. If Reynolds was the star of the movie, Frank Johnson was an extra, one of those hard-drinking sailors guaranteed to get into a brawl sometime during the picture, who ends up being hauled off by the shore patrol. He was a slight, slender man, only 5 feet 3 1/2 inches tall, weighing 128 pounds. He wore thick glasses, and almost all of his 15 missing teeth had been replaced by dentures. His formal education had ended after grammar school, and he was doing hourly work in a rubber factory when he enlisted as an apprentice seaman. As promised, that $32.60 a month pay the Navy was offering, plus all expenses paid, seemed like a fair deal.

Turned out, perhaps to his own surprise, Frank Johnson loved the Navy, loved it so much he reenlisted seven different times. He belonged: the Navy molded him and trained him to be a better man than he had imagined possible. They built up his physical presence and his self-confidence and brought to the surface parts of his personality that even he had never known existed. His size mattered far less than the growing number of stripes on his sleeve. People who otherwise might not have respected him obeyed those stripes.

The Navy turned him into a leader.

There were some rough seas along the way, though. Like Reynolds, Johnson began his career in China. It was there, while on the destroyer USS *Hulbert*, that he had the first of several scrapes with officers. The Navy also taught him to stand up for himself—and his men. The *Hulbert* was docked off the coast of Vietnam, in Cam Ranh Bay, when Seaman First Class Johnson was charged with "disobeying the lawful order of an officer," convicted and fined $10. That sentence was later tossed out by the Navy's judge advocate—because the actual offense was never set forth in the charge.

A few years later, while aboard the battle cruiser USS *Detroit*, he was again charged with being "disrespectful and contemptuous in manner and speech to an Officer," and sentenced to reduction in rank. But "in view of long and previous good record," that sentence was remitted.

Ship by ship, station by station, rank by rank, Frank Johnson established himself as an experienced, competent, reliable sailor, a good man who could be depended on in challenging situations. When something needed to be done, he figured out how to do it. When a catapult-launched floatplane went over the side of the cruiser USS *Raleigh* in choppy seas, for example, Boatswain's Mate First Class Johnson volunteered to be suspended from the deck to attach a hook to the plane, risking his life to successfully salvage it.

In March 1941, he was aboard the destroyer USS *Ludlow* when it was commissioned, serving through its fitting out and shakedown cruise. He was especially good at that, having helped put several new ships into service, including the destroyer USS *Macdonough* and, most recently, the *Essex*-class carrier *Yorktown*.

So it was not surprising he would be assigned to *Intrepid* in time for its christening. He joined the ship wearing the crossed anchors designation of a chief boatswain's mate.

As far back as the 1400s, "bosuns" have been performing and supervising the myriad tasks necessary to keep a ship functioning. A poem published in Intrepid's newspaper outlined the rank:

> *I think there's nothing quite so great*
> *Or lovely as a boatswain's mate . . .*
> *For the boatswain's mate is always right*
> *He's on the job both day and night.*
> *He shouts at us in line all day*
> *To square all hats and throw butts away!*

Basically, bosuns are the conductors who run the deck; the chief plans, schedules, assigns able seamen to do absolutely every conceivable task—then manages their work. Frank Johnson was especially good at this; during his 24 years in the Navy, he had done every one of the jobs he now supervised. He literally had swabbed the decks but also was a qualified gun captain on a destroyer.

Unlike many sailors, Frank Johnson was not a superstitious man. Nevertheless, he was fully aware that *Intrepid* was his 13th ship.

While veterans like Reynolds and Johnson had served on numerous ships, *Intrepid* was Richard Montfort's first sea duty. He never expected to be there. Montfort was 38 years old, too old to be drafted, and enjoying his career as an electrical engineer at New York's Consolidated Edison. He could have avoided the war and continued serving customers on the home front. For him, though, the Navy wasn't a career choice. It was a means to escape a failing marriage. Fortunately, there was a real need for men with his expertise the military.

Montfort was an experienced electrical engineer, a graduate of the highly regarded Bliss Electrical School. He could trace a short, thread a wire through the thick plaster wall of a New York City apartment, or keep an engine running—skills desperately needed in the rapidly growing Navy. As he stood in the back row of the ranks—placed there because, at 6 feet 2 inches, he was one of the tallest members of the new crew—more than anything he just wanted a cigarette. He wasn't interested in listening to long speeches. Actually, he didn't like short speeches either. He was anxious to get going, get the job done. There was a tremendous amount of work to be done. It was an awesome challenge. He had spent his entire career trying to keep live wires away from water, and now he was at least partially responsible for maintaining a complicated electrical system—in the middle of the ocean!

It hadn't taken Montfort long to adjust to Navy discipline, although he did miss his teenaged daughter and his Great Dane. In his work for ConEd, maintaining order was essential: you had to do it the same way, the right way, every time. There were no short cuts when safety mattered. One way of doing that, he had learned, was taking notes, writing everything down; that way, he had the information if he needed it. So he decided to keep a diary of his time in the service. "Ship christened. Captain Sprague spoke. Seems professional," he wrote that day.

After the ceremony ended, he changed into his work clothes and got to it.

While a token group of veterans like Reynolds and Johnson, aided by newbies like Montfort, were putting the ship through its final fitting out, sort of an ultimate test drive during which all the builder's imperfections are identified and repaired, almost 3,000 from every part of the country reported for duty or were attending onshore training schools in preparation for joining the crew. Creating an entire crew was a complex operation, like populating a small city able to provide every necessary service while fighting the war. Among those men were 25-year-old Gordon Gail Keith, a high school graduate and local football hero from the small hamlet of Milo, West Virginia, a town whose entire population was less than the crew of a carrier, who had enlisted in 1939; 18-year-old Ray Stone from Lawrence, New York, a bustling suburb on Long Island; and 21-year-old Jacob Elefant, from the streets of Canarsie, Brooklyn.

Gordon Keith came aboard from the light cruiser USS *Cincinnati*. He was a petty officer, basically the equivalent of an army corporal, meaning he did whatever task had to be done, but he also was assigned the unusual designation of ship's sailmaker. Few people were even aware that modern warships had a "sailmaker."

Gordie Keith would not be called upon to make or mend sails, but he was responsible for maintaining the thousands of yards of canvas used on a modern aircraft carrier for every task from hatch covers to, unfortunately, sewing the canvas shroud in which dead sailors were cast into the sea.

He knew how to sew, a skill that had been taught to him by his mother, who could make a dress or mend his pants on her Singer sewing machine. He could thread a needle and draw it through canvas. He knew the strongest stitches. The hope was that he would not be very busy. The reality was far more sobering.

Like so many thousands of young Americans, 16-year-old Ray Stone got in line and tried to enlist on December 8, 1941, and like so many of those young patriots, he was turned away because he was too young. A year later, after his parents signed the age waiver, he finally was able to join the Navy. After boot camp, he was sent to the Fleet Radar School in Virginia Beach, where he was taught to operate the new high-tech radar system being installed on carriers. While Gordon Keith was literally making *Intrepid* shipshape, Stone was learning "to operate different air and search radar sets . . . The SK model radar was state-of-the-art . . . It could pick up a single plane or group of planes 150 miles away . . . determine the speed and course of a target," and identify approaching aircraft as friendly or enemy.

Jake Elefant, the son of Polish and Hungarian immigrants, enlisted on his 21st birthday, September 11, 1942. A graduate of Brooklyn Technical High School, he was sent to the Navy's monthlong catapult school in Philadelphia. Catapults, which released stored tension to blast planes off a ship without using a runway, had become essential on the new carriers. Someone somewhere probably saw Elefant had graduated from a technical high school and figured he was a good fit.

After finishing catapult school, he was assigned to the new *Yorktown*—but by the time he got to Norfolk, that ship had already sailed. More than a million men and women had enlisted in the Navy in the months after Pearl Harbor. Boot camp—basic Navy training—had been shortened when necessary to as little as three weeks, but an extensive network of schools—like Stone's radar course and Elefant's catapult school—had been established to train sailors in the technical skills needed onboard. Through July and August, the *Intrepid*'s first crew, its "plank owners," reported to the Newport News Receiving Station to be welcomed aboard.

On August 15, Elefant wrote in his new diary in a neat cursive script, "Boarded the *Intrepid*." A day later he noted, "Ship was commissioned."

A commissioning ceremony is a formal event that denotes the Navy's official acceptance of a ship into active service. It means that the ship is fitted out and its officers and crew are trained, equipped, and prepared to fulfill its mission. The tradition in America dates back to December 1775, when Lieutenant John Paul Jones hoisted the first American flag, the historic "Flag of America," or Continental Colors, with its 13 alternating red and white stripes and British Union Jack on the Continental Navy's first ship, the USS *Alfred*. The

Alfred, a merchant vessel originally named *Black Prince*, had been purchased by the Continental Congress, converted into a 30-gun frigate, and renamed in honor of the ninth century English monarch Alfred of Wessex.

More than 20 years later, in February 1797, the Navy commissioned its first true warship, the three-masted frigate USS *United States*; Revolutionary War hero Captain John Barry was given command.

The *Intrepid* joined the battle fleet at one o'clock on the afternoon of August 16, 1943, at the Norfolk Navy Yard. In earlier years, the commissioning of a major warship would have been a glorious celebration, with all the expected pomp and circumstance. Not now. There wasn't time for it. Hundreds of new ships of every class were being launched as fast as they could be built. In fact, one day later, another new *Essex*-class carrier, the *Wasp*, would be launched at the Bethlehem Fore River Shipyard in Quincy, Massachusetts. Two weeks later at the Newport News yard, *Intrepid*'s sister ship, originally USS *Kearsarge* but renamed *Hornet*, was commissioned.

There also was wartime security to be considered. The enemy was watching—and reading the newspapers. Not a single story about *Intrepid*'s commissioning was published the next day. But a confidential Navy document dated August 16, 1943 reported: "Pursuant to the Vice Chief of Naval Operations . . . the USS *INTREPID* was accepted by the Navy and placed in full commission this date."

Traditions stretching back 150 years still had to be honored. Instead of festivities, the ship was welcomed with a somewhat somber ceremony. *Intrepid*'s 3,000-man crew, resplendent in their dress whites, were joined on the flight deck by more than 100 dignitaries in uniforms or summer suits, many of them accompanied by women in long skirts, hats, and gloves. The ship's newly organized band welcomed them with John Sousa's spirited marches and a medley of patriotic tunes.

Ironically, there were no aircraft aboard the aircraft carrier. Air Group 8 would land on its deck during the shakedown cruise.

Assistant Secretary of the Navy for Air Artemus Gates, one of the 30 Yale men who had formed the Navy's first aviation unit during World War I, gave the welcoming address. Gates was a true American hero; he'd gained national recognition during the Great War by removing his guns from his plane to save weight, then swooping down in enemy territory to rescue two British flyboys. Later in the war, he was himself shot down and captured by Germans; after a bold escape attempt—climbing through the window of a prison train in a tunnel—he was recaptured but released after the armistice.

Secretary Gates was a fine speaker and made the expected laudatory speech. There were a lot of thanks to be spread, and pride and wishes and hopes and prayers to be expressed. Then he conducted the traditional business, announcing several awards and citations and reading the commissioning directive appointing Thomas L. Sprague the first captain of USS *Intrepid*.

Tom Sprague followed by addressing his crew for the first time. This was a far more serious matter. Few of the men standing on that deck knew much about his ability to some-

Captain Tom Sprague on the bridge of *Intrepid* while at Majuro,
February 6, 1944. *Collection of the Intrepid Museum. 1943–1945 USS
Intrepid Cruise Book.*

how transform 3,000 men and 170 officers into a single cohe-
sive team. They knew his background. They knew he was an
aviation pioneer. They knew the posts he'd held on other ships:

navigator on the *Langley*, XO on the *Ranger*, commanding officer of the *Pocomoke*. They knew he'd taken the escort carrier *Charger* through its trials. No one doubted he knew all the ropes and knots—they wouldn't have given him this boat if he didn't—but they also knew this was his first major command.

For literally thousands of these sailors, this was their first ship. Sprague and the *Intrepid* would take them into the war—and they did not know what to expect.

Word gets around quickly in the military. Paths cross and recross. The scuttlebutt was that Sprague was a tough, fair, and highly competent skipper, a man you could trust. But beginning on that sunny August afternoon, their lives were in his hands. The odds were incredibly high they were going to get hit by the Japanese, and when that happened, his decisions would make all the difference. They wanted a leader with fight in him—an aggressive captain who would take the fight to the enemy, but do it in a manner that would bring them home. So they wanted to take his measure.

"We are now engaged in a great war," he began, his voice somber and touched with Midwestern earnestness. Sprague had given hundreds of speeches during his career, but none of them as important as this one. He was mercifully brief, as his men were standing in formation under the August sun. "Enemies from across the sea have attacked us without warning. They coveted the country for which our forefathers fought and died. They considered us incapable of defending ourselves. As has been said before, 'What kind of people do they think we are?'"

Sprague paused and looked up from his notes, allowing those words to hang in the air. He took those seconds to look at his men. He wondered about them, too. The responsibility that had been put on his shoulders was enormous. This crew was young and woefully inexperienced. Few of them had ever been in combat. They had been trained to perform all the mundane tasks necessary to keep the ship in fighting trim, but until they were in combat . . .

He took a deep breath, squared his shoulders, and continued. "This ship's company, assembled for the first time on these decks, appears to be a good and sufficient answer. Entrusted to our hands today is a fine ship. She has been honestly and skillfully built. It is now up to us.

"There is much work ahead. There are many problems to solve before *Intrepid* will be ready to meet the enemy and strike the powerful blows of which she is capable . . . We will get on with that job . . .

"No ship ever put to sea in time of war has had a better name than ours—*Intrepid*—fearless, bold, brave, undaunted, courageous . . ." he said each word firmly, ". . . resolute, valiant, heroic—these are the words which define our name." He paused once again before issuing a challenge. "Only in the cool courage and fearless bravery of the present crew, will the spirit of the heroic and undaunted crews of the past live again. Let us live and fight our ship by that name."

Sprague ordered both *Intrepid*'s ensigns hoisted: the American flag that would fly from the stern and the ship's red, white, and blue commissioning pennant. Then he set its first watch.

The ship's executive officer, the head of its air group, Commander Richard K. Gaines, said a few words. Gaines was an experienced combat veteran, having led flight operations on the *Enterprise* throughout the Solomon Islands campaign. "All hands have done a real Navy job in fitting our ship," he said. In contrast to Sprague, his speech was more of a rouser, and in his few words, he hit all the right patriotic notes. "We are ready to take her over. We are rarin' to go—to make every minute, from here on out, count toward developing the finest fighting team—officers, men, ship—that we are capable of.

"The enemy shall know well—in fear and trepidation—that we exist. *Intrepid*, a splendid name for a United States Naval vessel. 'All that the name implies' might well be our motto. And with this goal ever in sight we shall mete out proper punishment and thorough defeat to the enemy . . .

"*Intrepid*—the watch is set."

Following the official ceremony, Captain and Mrs. Sprague mingled on deck with the guests and crew. This was the kind of informal atmosphere that allowed him to greet some of his men, shake their hands, answer a few questions, tell some jokes, smile a lot, and display his charm. It wasn't just good ship politics, a bit of bonding. It was an opportunity he truly enjoyed. He wanted to know the men he was commanding, and believed it was vitally important to build the personal relationships that might someday make a difference.

He was good at it, too. Back at Annapolis, his classmates had wondered in their yearbook, "Did you ever hear a man laugh so heartily that it would spread to you, and make you laugh—even after a Juice exam? . . . [An unusually difficult test] There you have Duke. A laugh and a pleasant word when the world seems blue."

And if any of Captain Sprague's crew doubted his toughness, his classmates had some reassuring words for them: "Duke has a will of his own, but usually suppresses it until he gets sore. After that he suppresses the opposition."

The war was waiting. That morning's newspapers reported that six more ships had been lost in battle, including the destroyer *Maddox* and the submarine *Pickerel*. There was no estimate of casualties, although the stories noted somberly that those ships carried a total of 614 sailors.

A day later, the niceties done, *Intrepid* cast off its heavy lines and sailed into Chesapeake Bay for its first sea trials. In the next few weeks, a disparate group of sailors would be transformed into a crew. All the different talents they brought to this ship would be harmonized. They would test their equipment and learn how to make it sing. The first planes would land on its teak deck, and they would make a thousand or more practice takeoffs and landings. The deck crews—the airdales—would become proficient at moving planes around quickly, learning how to shave off the precious seconds that might make a difference in combat. The anti-aircraft guns would be fired and fired again and again at plane-towed targets or small, bright red drones. The mess would learn how to serve 3,000 hot meals two or three times a day. Sailors would brew hundreds of pounds of coffee beans every day and literally peel and cook a ton of potatoes for meals. Phil Reynolds's damage control crews practiced racing to their designated positions, rolling out hoses to put out multiple fires or plugging bomb holes in the deck. In the control room, officers and men would get a feel of her, how fast she turned, how she caught the winds, and how glorious she was when she so gracefully cut through the waves.

Captain Sprague seemed everywhere, cheering when necessary, demonstrating when appropriate, criticizing when deserved. Everybody heard his oft repeated message: "Don't practice your mistakes. Do it once and do it right."

There was much to learn. The first few days, people stumbled around the ship, trying to find the barber shop, the ready rooms, the chapel and the library, the dentist and doctors, but most importantly, the quickest route to their combat stations. Sailors got turned around. They got disoriented and lost in the maze of passageways. At times they spent hours wandering around searching for their own bunks.

The veteran hands taught the green kids. Chief Boson's Mate H.P. Crook liked what he saw. "Our men have had everything to learn but they retain what they learn. Unlike the enemy, they find out how to do their own thinking. Now they need practice; need to speed up at least 50%. They have to learn to observe the three fundamental rules rigidly: One, Get to your battle stations on the double; Two, Be alert when you get there; and Three, Observe 'smoking lamp out in darken ship periods.'"

For the young sailors, those first few days were an adventure. Everything was new and different. They watched. They learned. They got caught sneaking a cigarette when the ship was blacked out, not yet fully understanding how a small light in the middle of the night ocean could give away their position.

The men who had been in combat came down hard on them. This was no joyride; their lives were at stake.

Of course, they also taught them the subculture that has existed belowdecks throughout Navy history. They showed them how to filter the alcohol out of aftershave lotion through a loaf of bread—and a few secret stills were set up and opened for business. Small-stakes card games and craps were regularly scheduled. The tattoo artists set up their operations. But all of this served to bring sailors together.

Mistakes were made during these trials. One afternoon, for example, as torrential rain and high winds rocked the boat, in the combat information center, Ray Stone spotted an unidentified object on his new radar screen—racing directly toward the ship at, according to his calculations, an astonishing 75 knots. In a nor'easter!

It didn't seem possible. Nothing flew that fast. It had to be an equipment malfunction. But he remembered his training: never ignore a blip. Day after day in school, he was taught that. Never ignore a blip. Better to be wrong than dead. His commander reported to the bridge: "C.I.C. to Bridge: We have an unidentified flying object bearing down on the ship at about 75 knots. Over."

The bridge took it seriously. "Bridge to C.I.C.: Nothing flying in this weather. What do you think it is? Over."

"Bridge from C.I.C.: Have no idea. Maybe a flock of geese? Over."

"C.I.C. from Bridge: Did you say geese? Over."

Seconds later, a flight of geese was heard squawking above the din. The first "attack" on *Intrepid* had been successfully identified. As silly as it sounds, though, these incidents made a difference: clear and rapid communications between the spotters staring at their screens and the commanders on the bridge were absolutely essential. In combat conditions, a wasted few seconds might literally be a lifetime.

As the days and weeks passed, Captain Sprague shook 3,000 hands, learned more about his crew, emphasized training, training, training, and took creative actions to boost morale. He even managed to find an organ donor. Literally. When he discovered one of his officers, one of Rick

Gaines's flight instructors, was a virtuoso on the electric organ, Sprague set out to find a suitable instrument for him. As far as anyone was aware, no ship had its own organ and organist. *Intrepid* would be first. Sprague actually traveled to Washington and obtained official permission from the Navy to bring an organ onboard.

Now all he had to do was find an organ. That proved far more difficult than he had imagined. Hammond's first electric organ had been offered for sale only eight years earlier. Electric organs were expensive and, due to rationing, hard to obtain.

The funds needed to pay for an organ were collected. But Sprague just couldn't find one for sale. Finally, he learned that another member of the crew had an organ he would allow the ship to have so long as it was for use by the entire crew. The next time *Intrepid* docked, several men raced into the night, all the way up the Rappahannock Valley to the officer's home. They packed up the organ and brought it safely back to the ship.

The story of the donated organ, which also requested crewmen supply lists of their favorite songs, appeared in the ship's newspaper—which Sprague also founded. Originally titled just *USS Intrepid*, it offered a $5 prize to the crew member who could come up with a better name. No one ever collected the prize—although after the first few episodes a banner was added to the front page depicting the original ketch *Intrepid* alongside the carrier and declaring "Then, Now, Forever."

As it turned out, it was not the presence of the organ that helped build morale. It was the captain making the effort to get the organ. A small gesture made a big statement. The word was spreading throughout: *this guy Sprague is okay.*

It did not take long for the crew to begin taking pride in their new ship. In early September, 420 men from a variety of divisions set a record for all ships in the class in the difficult and unpleasant task of cleaning the ship's bottom in preparation for painting. Under Phil Reynolds's direction, they accomplished the task in two and a half days, breaking the previous record by a half day. This was, according to the newspaper, the crew's "first real accomplishment . . . but they may also put out their chest, figuratively speaking, for the job was not only done speedily . . . but much better than any previous ship engaged in such an operation at that yard."

Intrepid officially became an aircraft carrier on September 16, when Andrew McBurney Jackson Jr., commander of Air Group 8, had the honor of making the first landing on the ship. Every member of the crew not on duty stood alongside the deck to witness that historic first landing. Sprague turned his ship into a steady 20-knot wind, and Jackson Jr. put down his Grumman F6F Hellcat square in the center of the deck.

A loud cheer reverberated through the ship. *Intrepid* was in business.

That was followed over the next few weeks by more than a thousand takeoffs and landings, day and night, in every type of weather as the crew learned and practiced moving planes up and down from the hangar deck to the flight deck and into takeoff position, fueling them, starting them, shutting them down, stowing them below. And shaving seconds off each part of the process; any second might be the one that made all the difference.

The deck was awash with colored shirts to designate responsibility: the "airdales" who moved planes into takeoff

Intrepid off the east coast of Panama with Air Group 8 on board,
November 28, 1943. *Collection of the Intrepid Museum. P00.2013.01.06*

position and unfolded the wings wore blue T-shirts. The pur-
ple shirts removed the chocks holding the wheels in place. The
men wearing green handled the arresting gear that grabbed
hold of the plane hooks. Firefighters and ammunition loaders
wore red, and those wearing yellow shirts moved planes between the hangar deck and flight deck. They practiced over
and over and over. Among the conductors of this orchestrated
teamwork was Lieutenant Charlie Devens, the ship's celeb-
rity, who had pitched for Babe Ruth and Lou Gehrig's New
York Yankees for three seasons in the early 1930s.

Problems were part of the process. One plane captain, responsible for the maintenance of the plane, forgot to check
its fuel load and let his plane take off with an almost empty
tank. Its pilot had to be rescued when it ran out of gas. Inex-

perienced pilots missed the catch wire and barreled into the restraining fence. Planes banged wings. As Jake Elefant noted, "Our squadron is still very green . . . [Some of the pilots] have had only a few hours practice in the new 'hell diver.'" But over those weeks, the number of mistakes was reduced as the crew learned how to function. They listened when Charlie Devens told them that teamwork makes all the difference— even the mighty Babe knew that. And if it worked for him and Gehrig and Lazzeri and Dickey, it would work for this ship.

At the beginning of October, Sprague took *Intrepid*, with its newly painted hull and smoothly functioning crew, out of Chesapeake Bay into the Caribbean Sea and all the way to Trinidad—and then back home to Virginia. After the crew enjoyed a final few days of leave at home, on December 3, 1943, the Navy's newest aircraft carrier finally was ready to fight.

THREE

MEN WHO GO to sea have always taken with them the combined experience, knowledge, and wisdom of all who sailed before them. The crew of *Intrepid* had been given a technological marvel, the most modern warship ever built. They had been well-trained and given the tools to succeed; mechanical defects had been discovered and repaired. There was only one thing left to consider: luck.

Superstition has always played an important role for sailors. For centuries, seafarers were sailing into the unknown, and many of them believed their fate depended on appeasing the gods. So they respected omens and offered sacrifices and interpreted signs, providing at least a comforting sense of control over their fortune. For example, it was widely believed that killing an albatross would bring bad luck to a crew, and even landlubbers knew the Biblical warning, "Red sky at night, sailors delight; red sky in morning, sailors take warning."

But there are other superstitions handed down through the generations that are respected by wary sailors. While few Navy men would admit to subscribing to ancient sailing legends, they were aware of them and paid attention to them.

They knew that spotting dolphins in the ship's wake at the beginning of a cruise brought good luck, while it was bad luck to begin a voyage on a Thursday or Friday.

Ships gained reputations. During the War of 1812, a British cannonball ripped through the deck of the fighting sloop *Saratoga*, somehow releasing a gamecock from its cage. The bird celebrated its freedom by landing on a rail of the damaged ship and crowing loudly and, the crew believed, defiantly. Emboldened, they fought back and defeated the larger enemy fleet. From that moment on, *Saratoga* was considered a desirable ship.

Conversely, the frigate *Chesapeake*, suffered a serious of ignominious defeats during that war, including being captured in that same war after its captain, James Lawrence issued the memorable command, "Don't give up the ship." Cementing in history its reputation as an unlucky ship.

In the Navy, word got around pretty quickly which ships were considered lucky. Men would try to get aboard, while unlucky ships were avoided if possible. Bombs just missed lucky ships, while the flaming wreckage of destroyed Zeros crashed into unlucky ships. Not a single American carrier was at Pearl Harbor when the Japanese attacked. Was that luck?

A ship earns its reputation over time. Sailors take notice of small events. It is considered an ominous sign if the champagne bottle doesn't break during a christening ceremony. At *Intrepid*'s christening, it had taken three attempts before Mrs. Hoover successfully smashed the bottle. But finally, it did break. Was it an omen or not?

More ominous signs were soon to appear for the new ship. Through October into November, *Intrepid* completed its shakedown cruise. Problems were sorted out. Morale was built. In Port of Spain, Trinidad, Captain Sprague threw a beach party for the crew consisting, reported one crew member, of "food, athletics, beer and swimming." Milestones were reached: On October 23, Ensign R.D. Phipps made the thousandth landing on the ship. About a month later, as the ship headed to the coast of Maine for final trials, the crew celebrated its first Thanksgiving at sea. It was a melancholy event; it was impossible not to think about their families celebrating at home. Captain Sprague joined the crew for a turkey meal with all the trimmings, from giblet gravy to cherry pie, topped off with cigarettes and cigars.

A prayer was also printed on the menu: "Grant us, O loving Father, the daily strength of body and soul to . . . overcome our enemies and honor thee ever in justice and charity."

Tom Sprague had gotten the sense of his ship. The crew liked him, but more importantly, they trusted and respected him. They were content to go to war with him. His regular fitness report, filed by Admiral Bellinger, rated him "Outstanding . . . Such special classification is fully justified in the case of this officer. He possesses that rare combination of intelligence, personality and practical sense in a very high degree . . ."

"Practical sense" meant that he remained calm in challenging situations. Other reports praised his ability to quickly adapt to existing conditions and find creative solutions while maintaining mission control.

Sprague spent the last days of November conducting speed and maneuverability trials in the cold water of Maine's Boothbay, which matched the water temperature in the Pacific. It was time, finally, to let *Intrepid* off the leash, let her rip, loosen her reins, give her full head, see what she had under the hood, put the winds in her proverbial sails.

For those four days, *Intrepid* played on the waves, reaching speeds of almost 36 knots, cutting and turning and dashing and darting. Sprague and the crew learned how maneuverable she was, how she responded when asked for more—more speed, sharper turns. During these trials, the ship conducted damage control scenarios. In one of them, a portside engine shaft was locked, as if the propeller had been put out of action, while the two shafts on the starboard were given full power; the objective was to determine how to adjust the rudder to maintain a steady course. After experimenting with numerous options, it was determined that a rudder angle of 6 1/2 degrees was necessary to compensate for the loss of the engine to keep control of the ship.

They did not test for the total loss of rudder control. Although the mighty German battleship *Bismarck* had been disabled, then sent to the bottom in 1941 after British torpedo planes had jammed its rudder, that was considered an extraordinarily lucky shot and certainly not likely to be duplicated.

Intrepid sailed home for the final time. Sprague, Reynolds, Gaines, and the other officers had pushed hard, and the veterans aboard had seen the change in the greenies. They no longer wandered aimlessly through the corridors. They could make it from their bunk to their battle station—even in a battle-darkened ship—in seconds. Deck crews had become proficient in launching and recovering planes. Lookouts and gunners had become competent at instantly differentiating American planes from the enemy.

While no captain ever is completely satisfied, or even content with his ship and crew, Sprague was ready to take *Intrepid* to war.

The first *Essex*-class carriers, *Essex* and *Yorktown*, had sailed into combat three months earlier. Their performance, their ability to deliver a devastating punch, had been superb. Admiral Chester Nimitz, Commander in Chief of the Pacific Fleet and Pacific Ocean Areas, desperately wanted to add more of them as rapidly as possible. *Intrepid* was next.

American strategy against Japan was to hopscotch across the Pacific, destroying enemy ships and planes when possible, but more importantly capturing islands that could be used as airfields from which bombers could fly closer and closer to the enemy. Tiny specks on maps that few people had even known existed before the war had become historic battlegrounds: the Solomon Islands, the Marshall Islands, the Gilbert Islands, Guadalcanal, New Georgia, Bougainville, Tarawa, Makin. And while *Intrepid*'s first mission remained top secret, Sprague was ordered to join Operation Hailstorm, a massive task force gathering to attack Truk Lagoon.

The omens remained mixed, however. *Intrepid* left the East Coast, steaming south for the Panama Canal, on December 3, 1943. There was some grumbling from the crew. December 3 was a Friday. An unlucky day to set sail. Sunday, they said. Sunday is the day to begin a journey.

Sprague was a realist; there was no place for superstition during a war. The war wouldn't wait. Decades in service had taught him that bombs make their own luck.

The crew's fears were reinforced during flight operations two days later. While approaching the ship for a landing during anti-submarine exercises, the engine of an F6F fighter piloted by Ensign Bill Preston stalled. There was no obvious reason for it. It was a bright afternoon, the weather was perfect, and the plane gave no indication of trouble. It just happened. Suddenly. Unexpectedly. The Hellcat hit the water and sank within seconds. Preston never got out. It was *Intrepid's* first fatality.

What happened soon after might have caused even Sprague to wonder.

Five days later, *Intrepid* anchored in Colón, Panama's second largest city and the gateway to the canal. The crew did not yet know their mission, or where their ship was headed, but they knew they were going into combat. So they took full advantage of what many feared was a last liberty. Or, as some sailors described it, *join the Navy and see the girls.*

For some members of the crew, this was a revelatory experience: Like Gordon Keith, they were young, a significant number of them were under 21, and many of them had never traveled outside their local region. Panama opened a new world, exciting, exotic, enticing, and ready to fulfill their fantasies. They took full advantage of the opportunity.

A bonding experience, as Sprague would later refer to it. Fortunately, penicillin was readily available to clear up lasting memories.

At 0530 the following morning, *Intrepid* entered the first lock of the canal. The Panama Canal is a 50-mile-long cut through the Isthmus of Panama connecting the Atlantic and Pacific Oceans. At that time, it consisted of three large "locks," or steps. Ships entered a lock, which was then enclosed. The water level was raised or lowered to allow safe passage to the next step. The canal had opened in August 1914; President

Theodore Roosevelt had ordered it built after the Spanish-American War. It changed the world, cutting more than 7,000 miles and a month off the time it took a ship to sail between the great oceans.

It had opened with great fanfare, considered one of the great engineering marvels in history. "It makes five centuries of dreams come true," reported the *Oregon Daily Journal*. "It is America's crown of success upon Columbus' and Balboa's failure to find a way to Asia."

USS *Jupiter*, later to be decommissioned, then redesigned as the *Langley*, was the first Navy ship to transit the canal. More than a decade later, *Langley* would again slip through the canal to stage a surprise—Sunday morning mock raid on Pearl Harbor. In that war game exercise, 152 aircraft from the *Lexington* and *Saratoga* "attacked" the airfields and Battleship Row, dropping "bombs," sacks of flour, on the island. Supposedly, that "wake-up call" exposed Pearl Harbor's vulnerabilities, but in fact, it served as a playbook for the Japanese Imperial Navy.

Captain Sprague had passed through the Panama Canal for the first time during a summer cruise in 1915 as a midshipman aboard USS *Ohio*, one of the first battleships to use the canal. The trip through "the Ditch," wrote a classmate, took "four bells and a jingle." Since then, Sprague had gone through it several times without incident. In fact, he had filmed two previous trips through the canal on his Cine-Kodak home movie camera to give Evelyn and the kids a sense of the wonder of it. This time though, he did not have that luxury.

Phil Reynolds had been through the canal about half a dozen times, beginning more than a decade earlier. He always found something he hadn't seen before. He always enjoyed it. And he always had fun making up outrageous stories for the crew. When fresh flowers were available, he would toss one over the stern, explaining it was an offering to the water spirits. This trip, though, there were no flowers.

Intrepid had been designed to squeeze through the canal's 110-foot width with inches to spare. In fact, its portside deck edge elevator, which raised planes to the flight deck, was hinged so it could be folded up to make it through.

Still, it was a very tight squeeze. A somewhat rickety platform had been built on deck to allow the professional canal pilot, Captain Keith Tracy, sufficient visibility to steer the ship through the locks.

His remarks were punctuated by occasional guttural groans and steel screeches as the hull bounced and scraped the rock sides of the canal, damaging the new paint job. Eventually men would have to be lowered over the sides in chairs to touch it up. Sprague demanded his ship be maintained in tip-top shape.

Moving at about 6 knots, *Intrepid* passed through the Gatun Locks and across Miraflores Lake without incident. This was an experience to be savored, to be remembered; few of the young sailors had ever dreamed they would be passing through the great Panama Canal. They'd read about it in textbooks: *this is the kind of feat America is capable of accomplishing!* As many as a thousand men stood along the sides of the flight deck to watch the procedure. At times they could reach out and touch the rocky cliff. Dozens more stood in the wide-open forecastle—the ship's gaping jaw in which the anchor chains were stored—as if they were in a movie theater enjoying a travelogue of a ship sailing leisurely up a broad river. One of the ship's two chaplains, Lieutenant Timothy Herlihy, provided the narration. "If you look carefully," he informed the crew over the ship's loudspeaker system, "you may see crocodiles on either shore." Those men with Brownie cameras snapped photos to prove they had been there.

By 1100 the ship was moving slowly through the Gaillard Cut, a rocky 8-mile-long gorge created by excavating 96 million cubic yards of dirt and rock. This was the most difficult segment of the canal to navigate. The wake of large ships passing through the locks ahead pushed back into the cut, creating a wave that combined with natural tides to make passage through it unpredictable and dangerous.

What happened next was never satisfactorily explained. The ship was emerging from the cut, moving into a wider portion of the canal, slowly turning about 10 degrees to the left. Sprague was on the bridge, admiring Captain Tracy's calm direction.

Suddenly, the bow swung sharply to the right, to starboard—heading directly for the rocky wall. Captain Tracy reacted instantly, ordering the port engines stopped and increasing the speed of the starboard engines to 10 knots, trying desperately to regain control. But the ship continued sliding to the right side of the channel. "Drop the port anchor!" he commanded.

The men watching from the forecastle had been enjoying the bucolic scene. In an instant, without warning and seemingly without cause, the ship veered hard to the right. The rocky cliff loomed directly in front of them, *Intrepid* heading straight into it. The anchor crew heard the order: drop the port anchor. The *port* anchor. They responded, tossing away their cigarettes and releasing the anchor chains.

Intrepid with her bow aground on the channel wall in the Gaillard Cut, December 9, 1943. *Collection of the Intrepid Museum. Gift of the family of Captain Charles T. Fitzgerald USN (Ret). P2024.29.05*

The starboard anchor chains.

Tracy made one last desperate attempt to prevent the collision, shouting, "Two-thirds speed astern! Two-thirds speed astern!"

Too little. Much too late.

They had dropped the wrong anchor. It hit the water fast and hard. Rather than preventing the collision, the starboard anchor pulled the ship into the cliff.

Intrepid slammed into the canal wall. The ship shuddered. A long, screeching whine ripped through the afternoon as sharp rocks sliced into the hull.

Fortunately, the ship had reduced speed to less than 2 knots. But damage was done: a 4-foot-by-3 1/2-inch gash ripped open the bow. Hull plates buckled. Steel wrinkled. Tons of water began rushing into several compartments.

Intrepid drifted back off the cliff as if temporarily stunned. The ship came alive: sirens, bells, men racing to their stations. Phil Reynolds's damage control teams took charge. Within seconds, watertight doors were sealed. The few seconds of terror almost immediately gave way to calm competence. Reports were sent to the bridge from every area. A few sailors had been jarred off their feet, but other than a few cuts and bruises, there were no injuries. The damage to the hull had been contained.

Within minutes it was determined the ship was secure, although later, more than a few *Titanic* jokes would be told. The anchor was raised, and *Intrepid* completed its passage through the canal without further difficulty.

When the ship was moored off Balboa, divers examined the damage. In addition to the sliced-open hull, they found numerous dents, wrinkled steel, and several cracks, but nothing catastrophic.

Sprague was furious. How did this happen? Although *Intrepid* was under the command of the canal zone pilot, he was fully aware he would be held responsible. It was his ship. That's the way things worked in the service.

Rumors had been circulating that he was in line for a promotion. This was the type of mark on his record that could affect that. Within hours, he officially requested a board of inquiry be convened to determine the cause of the incident.

Intrepid tied up in Balboa while emergency repairs were made to her hull. The board met the next day. A senior canal pilot testified that the probable cause of the accident was an unanticipated back-wave. A large ship pushes water forward, creating a wave about as long as the ship itself. As the canal narrows, it forms a wall of water powerful enough to move the bow of the ship. In this instance, to starboard. In fact, a ship had left the lock at Pedro Miguel only an hour or so before *Intrepid* entered it.

The forces of nature meeting the wonders of engineering had created an unpredictable situation. Captain Tracy had responded by ordering the port anchor dropped. Whatever was happening the ship had to be stopped. For some reason—there was speculation that the men in the anchor chain room were momentarily stunned by the mammoth cliff looming in front of them—they had mistakenly dropped the starboard anchor. That pulled *Intrepid* to the right— directly into the rock wall.

Although, as one crewman recorded in his diary, "Went through the canal and ran into a mountainside . . . Damage pretty bad," the board exonerated everyone. No one was at fault. A confluence of unusual events had created an untenable situation.

Fate. Or, it was whispered, *bad luck.*

For the first time, uneasy members of the crew wondered if they were aboard what someone dubbed "the evil I."

Temporary repairs were made. *Intrepid* sailed to San Francisco, where the damaged plates would be replaced. During the trip, Sprague kept the crew busy, drilling them over and over and over. The air group's torpedo planes practiced by firing dummy fish at the ship while the crew practiced taking emergency measures to avoid them. As much as Sprague maneuvered, a few of them bounced harmlessly off the hull.

They caused no material damage, but as much as the men told themselves *Intrepid* was a fortress, that clunking sound reminded them how vulnerable they really were.

In late December, *Intrepid* went into dry dock at Hunter's Point, across San Francisco Bay. For a sizeable number of the crew, this was their first Christmas and New Year's Eve away from home. Sprague did as much as possible to fight their homesickness. Once again, he made a point of showing up unexpectedly at different division celebrations, joining loudly in singing Christmas carols, often accompanied by the ship's Hammond organ, and successfully ignoring violations of the Navy's strict rules about alcohol.

He had spent more holidays away from home than he could count, he told them. He knew what they were feeling. He shared those same feelings. But, he reminded them, they were there for a reason. They were fighting for the people they were missing. It was a cliché, he acknowledged, but that didn't make it any less true.

On New Year's Eve, he invited Reynolds, Gaines, and several other officers into the captain's cabin and poured snifters of brandy. "To our crew," he offered, holding up his glass, then tapped twice on his desk and added, "and to this lady on which we sail."

While they were at Hunter's Point, the "Dry I," as other people had begun referring derisively to her, welcomed movie star Mickey Rooney aboard for a visit. Rooney, one of the best known and most popular actors in the world, joined the ship's band, playing drums on several numbers—including the ship's unofficial fight song, "Hawaiian War Chant," which had been popularized by Tommy Dorsey's orchestra in the movie musical *Ship Ahoy*. The USO also staged a show onboard featuring Connee Boswell, one of the famed Boswell Sisters, who sang her big hit, "Nobody's Sweetheart," as well as acrobats and jugglers.

In early January, repairs completed, *Intrepid* finally arrived in Pearl Harbor. They followed *Yorktown* into the port. "What a sight to behold," Jake Elefant wrote. "There were ships, ships and more ships of every type imaginable." There were carriers, battleships, destroyers, cruisers, submarines, and countless cargo ships, tenders, and oilers. Pearl Harbor had become the staging point for the Pacific war and was overflowing with ships, planes, supplies, and men.

But it also remained a graveyard. Most of the ships that had been hit on December 7 had long ago been raised, repaired, or discarded. Not all of them, though. *Intrepid* docked at the berth that had been occupied by the battleship *Tennessee* during the attack. The *Tennessee* had been lucky. It had been hit by two bombs but was back in service within months. Close by, though, were the remains of USS *Arizona*. *Arizona* had been hit by at least eight bombs, one of which ignited the munitions and fuel onboard, causing a massive explosion. The ship settled on the bottom, taking with it 1,177 men.

A portion of its bridge remained visible above the waters of the harbor. Officials had elected to leave the superstructure there: a tomb, a tribute, and a reminder. A continuous stream of oil bubbles rose from the wreckage as if *Arizona* were still breathing, Hundreds of *Intrepid*'s crew members stood silently at the railing as the ship glided by, removing their caps. A few men saluted or held their hands over their hearts. Surely some of them prayed. Until that moment, for many of them, the war had been an abstract concept. A distant reality. They might have even known people—relatives, friends, or neighbors—who had been killed or wounded or were missing. They certainly had heard combat stories from veteran shipmates. But this, this was different. It was impossible to look at that grotesquely twisted metal and not reflect on the men who lay below the surface forever.

This was the reality of war.

It was getting closer.

While in Hawaii, the inexperienced Air Group 8 was replaced onboard by Air Group 6, a significantly more experienced outfit that had seen a lot of action on the *Enterprise*. Air Group 6 was led by legendary pilot Hank Miller, the man who had taught Jimmy Doolittle's B-25 bomber crews how to take off from the *Hornet*. Among Air Group 6's pilots was Lieutenant Al Vraciu, who had been Medal of Honor recipient Butch O'Hare's wingman. The squadron had fought at Midway, Guadalcanal, and the Gilbert Islands. The ship's newspaper reported, "This group went through takeoff maneuvers and landings with deadly precision and machine-like accuracy that was thrilling to watch. Here were a bunch of men to be proud of, men who knew their business to the last detail."

That was reassuring. The safety of the ship would depend on these men. "Boy," Elefant noted with appropriate awe, "these pilots we've got now are sure hot."

On January 16, *Intrepid* eased out of Pearl Harbor, once again passing the *Arizona*. Just off Oahu, the ship joined the *Essex* and the light carrier *Cabot*, the battleships *North Carolina*, *South Dakota*, and *Alabama*, the antiaircraft cruiser *San Diego*, 10 destroyers, a submarine screen, and escort vessels that had come together to form Task Force 58. It was the most powerful naval armada ever assembled, capable of putting almost 700 planes in the air. The crew didn't know where they were heading, but wherever it was, it would be big-time.

Task Force 58 split into four smaller task groups, each of them including three carriers.

The big question remained: *Where are we going?* That was answered by Captain Sprague once they were at sea. "Now hear this," he began. "To all hands of the *Intrepid*, this is the Captain speaking." His voice flowed down corridors, penetrated from the bottom of the engine room to the top of the island. Immediately all work aboard ship ceased. This was what they had been waiting for, training for. "The greatest task force of carriers, battleships cruisers and destroyers ever assembled in the world and the greatest number of auxiliary vessels ever assembled in the Pacific, will strike Japanese bases in the Marshall Islands, commencing January 29th."

The Marshall Islands. Those men with access to maps tried to find them as Sprague continued. "The Marshall Islands . . . were given to Japan under the League of Nations mandate of 1920 . . . The islands were to be kept unfortified. No League observers, however, were allowed in the mandated islands . . . so they gradually became known as the Islands of Mystery. We know all too well that the nonfortification rule was not observed."

Sprague spoke in a matter-of-fact voice, a friend giving a history lesson. The Marshall Islands, he continued, were a group of coral atolls 2,500 miles from Japan and 2,100 miles from Pearl Harbor. In fact, the Marshall Islands consisted of

The pilots in the ready room get their instructions prior to the bombing run on the Marshall Islands. *Collection of the Intrepid Museum. P00.2012.01.13*

29 coral atolls, roughly circular islands or reefs surrounding a protected lagoon, and five coral islands. It was 66 miles long, 18 miles across. Its only real importance was as a military base. Its landlocked lagoons served as refueling and repair bases for the Japanese navy. "Until we have captured the Marshall Islands, the United States task forces will not be free from air attacks . . . in the western Pacific."

Due to its strategic importance, it was known to be heavily fortified; at least 100 warplanes were based there, probably even more, which "accounts for the tremendous force we are throwing against them at this time. This will be the first time we are making a large-scale attack at the pre-Pearl Harbor Japanese Empire."

The first time. The first time. The crew knew precisely what the captain meant. They had been talking about it since leaving Portsmouth. In the years since Pearl Harbor, America had been fighting a defensive war. The ships and the men who had been fighting for two years had blunted Japanese aggression. Now, Sprague was telling them, they were going on offense. That was incredible news. This was first stepping stone towards Japan, towards the end of the war in the Pacific, towards victory, towards going home.

"Our targets will be Kwajalein Atoll . . . the most important Japanese military and naval base in the Marshall Islands. [The island of] Roi is the target for the Intrepid planes."

In his diary, Chief Warrant Officer Richard Montfort wrote that day, "Getting ready for trouble. No one seems scared, in fact everyone seems as if this is what they have been waiting for. None want to back out now."

Montfort had been aboard *Intrepid* since the April christening ceremony, from the cold waters of Maine to the blistering heat of Trinidad to the collision in the canal. As an electrical engineer, he knew just about every foot of the thousands of miles of wiring that kept the ship alive. He had traced down electrical shorts, checked and rechecked the essential connections to the gun tubs, and dealt with the balky generators. Until this announcement, it had been all preparation and practice.

Now it was time to perform. As the ship sailed into combat, the crew tightened up. The watches were more alert. Men slept with their fireproof gear next to them. Training continued throughout the day and night. Anyone looking for a good omen, a positive sign that the Fates were paying attention, got one early on the night of January 20. *Intrepid* was powering through the Pacific at 22 knots when suddenly she came to an abrupt stop. The reason became instantly clear: *man overboard!* During night flying exercises, a radar-equipped fighter had gone into the water. The pilot was out there somewhere.

Finding one man floating in the ocean at night is like threading a needle in a dark room.

They waited. Ten minutes. Twenty. Thirty. Then, incredibly, a destroyer spotted the blinking red lamp on the pilot's life preserver. It was an improbable rescue. A sign.

On the 22nd, *Intrepid* crossed both the equator and the International Date Line. Normally, this would have been a day of celebration, a day "polliwogs," sailors crossing the equator for the first time, were welcomed into the Solemn Mysteries of the Ancient Order of the Deep with a raucous celebration. But not this time. This was not a time for frivolity; as Montfort wrote, echoing the sentiments of many of his crewmates, "I don't think this is much of a time to play around, especially with the ship being only 500 or 600 miles from enemy bases . . . playing around isn't my idea of doing something to finish this mess . . ."

Instead, Captain Sprague postponed the ceremony for two weeks. His message was simple: *we will celebrate after we take care of business.*

The waiting was hard. There were signs that the enemy was nearby: on the 24th, a destroyer on the protective screen made contact with a Japanese submarine, but it disappeared before its exact location could be determined.

The watch scanned the skies; in the CIC, Ray Stone and his shipmates hunched over their radar screens, but the enemy did not appear. Where was he? What was he doing? "We're wondering what's wrong with [them]," Elefant wrote. "They haven't sent a plane out to meet us. Could be they don't know we're coming." Or, far more ominously, they were holding back, preparing their own surprise.

It was impossible to think about anything else. Those men who had been in combat knew what to expect—they had been tested—but most of the crew wrestled with the one question soldiers had asked on the eve of their first battle for thousands of years: How will I respond?

Stephen Crane best described it in his Civil War novel *The Red Badge of Courage*: "So at last they were going to fight. On the morrow, perhaps, there would be a battle, and he would be in it . . .

"He had, of course, dreamed of battles all his life—of vague and bloody conflicts that had thrilled him with their sweep and fire. In visions he had seen himself in many struggles . . . A little panic-fear grew in his mind. As his imagination went forward to a fight, he saw hideous possibilities. He contemplated the lurking menaces of the future and failed in an effort to see himself standing stoutly in the midst of them."

The crew found ways to keep busy. They checked and rechecked equipment. They made sure they knew where their protective vests and helmets were at all times. They smoked. No one wandered farther than 30 seconds from their general quarters station. Hatches were battened down. Only escape hatches were used. Gun crews moved in and out of their tubs. Messages for the enemy—"This is for the *Arizona*" or "Eat this, Hirohito"—were scribbled in chalk on bombs before they were loaded. Plane crews stayed near their planes, some of them sleeping under a wing. Pilots waited in their ready rooms.

On the 27th, the cruiser *Indianapolis* joined the task force. Oilers spent much of the day refueling the warships. Still, no enemy planes or submarines were spotted, although late in the afternoon, without any explanation, a destroyer dropped several depth charges.

The next night, radar picked up four ships almost 30 miles away. Ours? Theirs? A destroyer went to investigate. Sprague kept the crew informed: *Unidentified ships have been spotted. Hold tight.*

They were Japanese supply ships. The destroyer fired the first shots of the attack. All four ships were quickly sunk. Did they spot the task force? Did they have time to warn the garrison on Roi and Kwajalein?

The attack was scheduled to begin at 0600 on the 29th. "The preparations are over," read Commander Gaines's Plan of the Day, which was distributed to the entire crew, "and we are now streaming at high speed for our launching point . . . To the best of our knowledge the presence of our force is still undetected by the enemy . . . At 0600 the *Intrepid* launches its first strike—21 dive bombers and 8 fighters. At 0715 we send off 12 Torpedo planes, each loaded with a 2,000-pound message. These will be dropped on runways . . ."

Intrepid had been imagined and built for one purpose: to put airplanes in the sky. It had taken years to turn that blueprint into reality. That day had finally arrived. The bombers would have fighter escorts. Other F6F Hellcats would remain above the island to greet enemy planes. An antisubmarine patrol and a security screen for the task force would be continuously airborne. Enemy bases throughout the Marshall Is-

The first torpedo bomber to land on *Intrepid*'s deck, September 16,
1943. *Collection of the Intrepid Museum.* P00.2012.01.07

lands would be simultaneously attacked by planes from other
carrier groups.

   "We have an exciting schedule to meet," Gaines's announcement continued, "one which is timed to the minute
with those of *ESSEX* and *CABOT*. This is the chance we
have been waiting for. LET'S GO *INTREPID!*"

Intrepid's targets were the airfields, installations, and depots on the islands of Roi and Namur.

It was a promising dawn. As had been predicted, the weather was good. At 0530, the task force turned into the prevailing wind at about 20 knots, generating a strong headwind to assist takeoffs. A Hellcat was the first plane off *Intrepid*'s deck, precisely at 0600. Hellcats had been in service only six months, replacing the slower F4F Wildcat—long enough for pilots to have fallen in love with it. "If they could cook," declared one of them, "I'd marry one."

Captain Sprague was on the bridge, watching the planes being launched. As that first Hellcat dipped slightly below the deck, then surged powerfully into the air—and wiggled its wings to salute the crew—he glanced at Phil Reynolds, clenched his fist, and shook it. *Here we go.*

Reynolds nodded. "Congratulations, Skipper," he said. It had been seven months since Sprague had walked up the gangplank in Newport News onto the unfinished ship. His ship. He had supervised its completion, welcomed the 3,000-man crew, taken it through training, tests, and trial—and the tribulation in the canal—and sailed it into combat. It had been christened and commissioned, but this was its baptism.

He raised his binoculars and watched the symphony being played on deck; all that training was paying off. Planes were moved rapidly into position and took off, with that spot filled within seconds by the next plane and then the next plane. The Hellcats, then the Avengers and Douglas Dauntless dive-bombers roared off the deck, dipped, then lifted into the air.

Sprague appreciated the beauty of a fully loaded carrier roaring into action. How many thousands of takeoffs and landings had there been in his career? Either in the cockpit or watching wistfully from the bridge? He once had tried to calculate, make a reasonable guesstimate. It was impossible. A lot, he decided, a lot.

Air Group 6 had been unleashed. After the last plane took off, the deck became eerily silent. There was nothing to do but scan the skies and wait. The airdales cleaned up, removing chocks, putting fuel lines away. The rest of the crew remained at general quarters in case the enemy responded. XO Rick Gaines popped into the CIC. Once his planes were airborne, that became their control room. Lots of blips were showing on radar screens. The operators confirmed: all friendly.

This already had been one of the most exciting days of Gordon Keith's life—and it was still only midmorning. The only other ship he'd been on, the light cruiser *Cincinnati*, had sailed back and forth across the Atlantic escorting convoys. A lot of long and pretty boring days. Not like this morning.

Keith was working in the canvas storeroom on the starboard side of the third deck. He was in the bowels of the ship, assigned to Commander Reynolds's Hull Department, so there was nothing for him to see. He had spent more than an hour that morning checking to confirm that all the paint—which had been found to emit noxious gases during a fire—had been chipped off the bulkheads. But the thunder of the planes taking off rumbled throughout the entire ship. During two flight training exercises, he'd managed to get up on deck—the captain was good about that as long as you weren't on duty and stayed well out of the way—so he could visualize what was happening. It was pretty impressive the way the handlers moved those planes around the crowded deck so quickly, so easily, and so safely.

Normally he didn't mind working below. It could get bitterly cold at sea in the winter, colder than the West Virginia hills, so being out of the weather was a good thing. But being down there during combat operations made him uneasy. That was something new. He'd been wondering how that would feel, and now he knew: helpless. Turned out a lot of guys felt that way. They had talked about it. You didn't know what was happening until it had already happened. By that time, it might be too late.

So you paid sharp attention to any unusual sounds—and you always knew where the nearest escape hatch was located. There wasn't much else you could do. Pray, maybe.

He stayed on edge. The crew had been ordered to battle stations several times in the last few days, all false alarms. And like just about everyone else, he wondered, what happened to the Japanese?

That was the big question. Where was the enemy? No one was complaining, but it wasn't much of a fight. "What a dull battle we're having," Montfort mused in his diary. Word spread quickly throughout the fleet when a patrol plane reported sighting a submarine periscope. The destroyer *Sterett* raced to the coordinates—and found a buoy floating there. Hours later a single enemy bogey appeared on radar—the *North Carolina* and *Alabama* opened up, and it quickly disappeared.

The enemy had been completely surprised. A total of 122 Japanese planes were caught on the ground. The concrete runways on Roi were bombed in the first minutes, making it almost impossible for enemy planes to get off the ground.

In the afternoon, a few Japanese "Bettys," bombers, probably from bases on other islands, wandered into the area. They were flying ducks for *Intrepid*'s veteran pilots. Al Vraciu shot down three of them. Added to his two previous kills earlier in the war, that made him the ship's first ace.

At 1919 that night, the battleships and cruisers opened fire on the island from 20 miles away. Among them were several ships that had been sunk or damaged at Pearl Harbor. Their big guns pounded the island relentlessly for two days.

On the rainy morning of February 1, the largest amphibious assault of the war began as troops from the 4th Marine Division and the Army's 7th Infantry Division landed on the beaches of Kwajalein, Roi, and Namur. *Intrepid*'s Air Group 6 provided close support, hitting targets called out by the troops on the ground.

The three days of shelling, bombing, and strafing had been effective. Resistance was light. Only one enemy pillbox was left intact and functioning on the beach. It was later estimated as many as three quarters of the 8,500 Japanese troops on the islands had been killed or wounded. By the end of the day, Roi was secured; it took four days to wipe out all opposition on Kwajalein, the largest atoll in the world. An estimated 350 Americans had been killed or were officially missing in the fighting.

During those three days, Air Group 6 had flown almost 650 sorties and was credited with 12 enemy planes shot down and 43 more destroyed on the ground. It had sunk five ships and was believed to have sunk an additional five; two more were damaged. There was no count of the structures destroyed or damaged.

During the attack, enemy antiaircraft fire had shot down nine of *Intrepid*'s planes; three pilots were killed, the others and their crews were recovered. Once more, it turned out, survival was simply a matter of luck. An inch one way or the other. The official reports made it clear few planes had escaped without any damage. They limped back to the carrier with "Bullet holes in wing . . . Bullet holes in stabilizer . . . in port elevator . . . in fairing and vertical fin . . . in fuselage . . . starboard wing . . . windshield . . . rudder." One Avenger had lost its hydraulic fluid, so when the pilot attempted to land, he hit the brakes and "it lurched to the left and went over the side." The radioman/ bombardier and the turret gunner managed to get out before it crashed into the sea—but the pilot was lost.

There was a single fatality aboard ship. An accident. On the 29th, a plane handler on the flight deck turned the wrong way and was hit by a propeller; his skull was fractured. He died a day later. At dusk on the 31st, he was buried at sea. A Marine guard, the ship's officers, and almost a thousand men turned out for the ceremony on the deck edge elevator. After a priest concluded the prayers, a Marine honor guard fired several rounds. The crew stood at attention and saluted as "Taps" was played and the body slid into the deep.

A day later, a Hellcat blew a tire while taking off and went over the port side, taking with it several 20mm guns. The plane sank instantly, and once again, the pilot was lost. Death was coming more frequently now; the crew was getting used to it. Each time the shock was a little less. More often than ever before, "Did you know him?" was becoming a commonly asked question.

The battle for the Marshall Islands was over. It was a major victory. Sprague was elated, although he maintained his calm demeanor. After his decades-long career, this had been his first day, and night, commanding a ship in combat. He had been careful to maintain the calm, professional demeanor as an example to his men. No matter what he was feeling inside—and he would never admit to being a little jittery—the crew never doubted he was in charge of the moment. They could depend on him.

Intrepid had done its job. He was justifiably proud, telling the crew, "The personnel of all departments performed their duties with unity of purpose and precision. Considering that this was the first engagement of this vessel since its commissioning . . . with the enemy, the performance of all hands is considered to be especially meritorious. Well done."

Late on the afternoon of February 4, *Intrepid* sailed gracefully into Majuro Lagoon, the major anchorage in the Marshall Islands. It is about 20 miles in circumference and 5 miles wide. The Germans had used it as a naval base during the first World War. The carriers *Enterprise, Yorktown, Essex, Saratoga,* and *Bunker Hill* were already moored there, as well as numerous battleships, cruisers, destroyers, and supply ships. Only weeks earlier, the Japanese fleet had been there, but five days before the attack, it had departed.

No one knew precisely why.

Captain Sprague granted his crew a brief liberty. Each man was issued two cans of warm beer or warmer Coke and ferried ashore. There actually was no "ashore." Majuro was a coral island with literally nothing left standing after the American attack. Nothing to see, nothing to buy. And no women. Mostly it was brutally hot. Ray Stone recalled, "With no shade, you soon marched fully clothed into the water, after tucking your wallets and cigarettes into your hat and sat there submerged up to your chin. It was a ludicrous sight, hundreds of heads with white hats barely above the surface."

Even before *Intrepid* departed the next day, Navy construction battalions, the Seabees, had arrived and begun work repairing runways and restoring the buildings, the infrastructure needed to maintain the island as a forward military base.

The first fighter squadron landed there on February 12 and immediately began attacking Pacific islands closer to Japan.

The enemy had been caught unprepared, but it gathered forces from other islands and began fighting back. Within days, waves of Japanese bombers attacked Roi, killing or wounding 102 men.

But by that time, *Intrepid* was gone, on its way to a meeting with fate.

FOUR

INTREPID **HAD BEEN** tested and passed with its colors flying. The crew didn't kid themselves—they had enjoyed only a taste of combat—but still, it was delicious. A largely green crew now had experienced success; much of their battle anxiety had been replaced with confidence. They had done the job. They had put their planes into the air and delivered havoc to the enemy. And that was all that mattered.

The attack on the Marshall Islands was in the history books. It was time to tell the stories, write the poems, and prepare for the next fight. During the massive assault, only two ships in the task force, the 35,000-ton battleships *Washington* and *Indiana*, suffered any significant damage. And even that was not the result of enemy action.

On February 1, under the cover of a moonless night, *Indiana* was refueling four destroyers when its captain, James M. Steele—without signaling his intention to the task force—suddenly and inexplicably ordered a turn to starboard.

In the darkness, he did not see the *Washington*, steaming at 15 knots 1,500 yards off his right flank.

It was a disastrous maneuver. By the time *Washington* grasped the danger, it was too late. *Washington*'s officer of the

deck made a desperate effort to avoid the collision, screaming, "All stop. All back emergency. " The helmsman turned
hard left. Two blasts of the whistle alerted the crew, *stand by
for collision.*

There just wasn't enough ocean between them to avoid
the collision. *Washington*'s bow ripped into *Indiana*'s hull. The
impact was heard thousands of yards away. *Washington*'s bow
collapsed, destroying 60 feet of the forward hull; *Indiana* lost
more than 200 feet of armor plating.

Damage control took over; both ships were in jeopardy.
Indiana had been badly damaged at its most vulnerable point;
only one bulkhead on its third deck was keeping the hull
intact. In those first few minutes, no one knew if it would
hold; if it collapsed, the ship might be lost. Damage crews
raced to shore it up.

It held. *Indiana* was saved.

Ten men were killed: six aboard the *Washington*, four on
Indiana.

Tom Sprague knew Jim Steele. Their paths had crossed
briefly for the first time two decades earlier at flight school
in Pensacola, where Steele was an instructor. They had risen
through the ranks together and had several mutual friends and
many service acquaintances. Steele was a fine officer; he had
been in command of the *Utah* when it was sunk on December 7 and supervised its recovery. Having suffered through
his own incident in the Panama Canal, Sprague had a pretty
good idea what Steele was going through. But there wasn't
anything he could do to ease the pain. Few things are more
devastating to a captain than losing his men. Sprague could
recite the name of every sailor lost under his command. Men

had died in the night, and as *Indiana*'s captain, that was Steele's responsibility.

Testifying at a board of inquiry hearing several days later, Steele admitted being out of position when the collision occurred; he was relieved of his command and assigned to a desk on shore.

Sprague knew that accident was the end of Steele's Navy career. He didn't discuss it with Reynolds or Gaines, but he was pretty sure they were wondering the same thing: What the hell happened out there? How did an experienced captain like Steele make such a costly mistake? Ten men. Ten men had died. There were a lot of factors. Refueling at night without lights or radio communications was always complicated and dangerous, but still? And in the back of his mind—and he was certain every other commander shared the same thought—he feared: *Could it happen to me?*

The only answer was increased vigilance. *Make sure it doesn't happen.*

After the exhilaration of battle, normalcy felt temporary. As if they were faking it. A brief pause until the next battle. As the fleet rearmed and refueled, *Intrepid*'s crew found ways to fight the boredom. Some mail finally caught up to the ship—several of the men received long overdue Christmas cards. Almost everyone wrote letters home or to their sweethearts to assure them they were okay. Basketball and volleyball games were organized on the elevator. A lot of games were played—poker, acey-deucey, and cribbage were especially popular—and some dice were rolled. The entertainment committee traded movies with different destroyers, and the new films were shown in several places on the ship. Several men used buckets to try to catch the large jellyfish that filled the lagoon. There was nothing to do with them—those jellyfish are inedible—but catching them required a steady hand and some luck. Another group shot clay pigeons off the flight deck.

There were some distractions. The line and pulley used to transfer a sailor from a destroyer to the ship had accidently been rigged backwards, so there was great amusement as the man was pulled across—hanging upside down.

But most of the conversations were spent guessing where they would go next. It was a big ocean. "We didn't know where we were going," pilot Bob Bloomfield said, "but we knew we were going west, towards Japan." Betting pools were set up. Several men wagered they would be ordered back to Pearl.

They were wrong.

After Task Force 58 had weighed anchor, its commander, Admiral Raymond Spruance, met with all his air group leaders—including Rick Gaines—aboard *Yorktown*. When Gaines got back to *Intrepid*, he gathered his flight crews in the ready room and smiled confidently as he told them, "It's Truk."

Truk. Rather than returning to Pearl Harbor, Admiral Nimitz had decided to launch a surprise attack on Japan's most important forward naval base in the South Pacific. It was an audacious and dangerous decision. Truk Lagoon was heavily fortified. There would be substantial casualties. But it was a risk worth taking. Capturing Truk would eliminate a major enemy stronghold while providing a deep and safe harbor.

Nimitz assembled the largest carrier task force in history. Task Force 58 was comprised of 9 carriers, 7 battleships,

10 cruisers, 28 destroyers, numerous submarines, and dozens of supply ships. It was capable of putting 600 planes in the air.

Long forgotten were the debates of the 1920s and '30s about the strategic value of aircraft carriers. That question had been settled.

The *Langley*, America's first carrier, had been converted into a seaplane tender in 1937. Then Lieutenant Commander Sprague had been aboard throughout the entire transition. He had watched history give way to necessity. When the transition was completed, he had been transferred to *Saratoga*.

In February 1942, *Langley* was attacked by Japanese bombers off the Australian coast and was scuttled. As the crew was abandoning the historic ship, its radioman tapped out its last message: "Mama said there would be days like this. She must have known."

Unlike the Marshall Islands attack, there would be no landing troops on Truk. Operation Hailstone, as it was named, was not an invasion. Truk was to be decimated from the air and sea. The task force would wreck it, turn it into a wasteland, leave it devastated and useless, then bypass it to invade and occupy other islands.

In early February, two Marine Corps PB4Y-1 Liberators equipped with specially designed high-altitude cameras had secretly flown over the lagoon. Their photos revealed a significant number of warships—carriers, battleships, and destroyers from the Imperial Japanese Navy's 4th Fleet—anchored there, in addition to more than 100 planes. Nimitz hoped to draw the outgunned Japanese fleet out of the lagoon, confident his men would destroy it.

Back in the States, few people had ever heard of a place called Truk; within a week, it would be in the headlines of every American newspaper. The crews and pilots in Task Force 58 didn't know much more about it than the civilians—except that it would be heavily defended. Some of them would die there. "They didn't tell us where we were going until we were well under way," remembered Phil Torrey, commander of Air Group 9 aboard *Essex*. "They announced our destination over the loudspeaker. It was Truk. My first instinct was to jump overboard."

Even 5th Fleet Commander Admiral Marc Mitscher admitted later, "All I knew about Truk was what I'd read in the *National Geographic*."

They learned as much as possible in an effort to make it less mysterious, less menacing. Truk, or Truk Lagoon as it appeared on some maps, was part of an island group originally known as the new Philippine Islands, which had been discovered by Spanish navigator Álvaro de Saavedra in 1527. Almost two centuries later, this island group was renamed the Carolines after King Charles of Spain. In 1899, Germany had purchased the Caroline, Mariana, and Marshall Islands from Spain but lost them to Japan following the Great War. Although the Japanese agreed the islands would not be fortified, they refused to allow any inspection. What took place there had remained secret from the world.

Rather than a single land mass, Truk consisted of about two dozen islands in a beautiful lagoon, surrounded by 140 miles of barrier reef. There were only a few places in the reef deep enough for ships to enter the lagoon, and those positions were defended by a well-entrenched garrison. Reportedly, there were five airfields and one seaplane base spread among the islands. It was rumored that several hundred Zeros and Bettys were there, ready to protect the island against a carrier attack.

American intelligence was spotty. Beyond those few photographs, no one really knew what was waiting for the task force. The Japanese might be dug in, heavily fortified, and ready to fight to the last defender. Or, conversely, assuming they had no early warning and the Imperial fleet was still there, with a little luck, this just might be Japan's Pearl Harbor.

The task force did get some luck: rain squalls had shielded its approach.

The only aspect of the attack that made *Intrepid*'s crew wary was the fact that it was to begin before dawn on the 16th. Sixteen was a mystical number in *Intrepid*'s history. It was on February 16, 1804, that the first *Intrepid* under Stephen Decatur's command slipped into Tripoli Harbor and set fire to the *Philadelphia*. On May 16, 1892, the second *Intrepid*, a 330-ton steamer, had been sold and stricken from the Navy list. Supposedly, while this fourth *Intrepid* was under construction at Newport News, two welders had been seriously injured in an accident on the hangar deck—on April 16, 1943. This ship had been commissioned on August 16. And now they were getting ready to launch a major attack—on the 16th.

Probably just a coincidence. Few people took any of that stuff seriously. But still . . .

The attack began at 0645. Seventy-two Hellcats took off from their carriers, gathered in formation over the task force, and headed for Truk. Their mission was to destroy Zeros, clearing the skies for the slower, less maneuverable bombers and torpedo planes to hit the island. The Hellcats flew in low, exploiting a flaw in Japanese radar. The defenders were stunned; the attack was a complete surprise.

But the Americans were surprised, too. The intelligence had been wrong. The Japanese had spotted the reconnaissance planes and ordered their warships to Palau, an island group 1,200 miles away—leaving behind a lagoon filled with tankers and freighters and a few cruisers.

The intelligence also was wrong about the number of planes the attackers would face. In their briefing, pilots had been told there were slightly more than 100 aircraft on the island. In fact, 365 planes were based there.

Luckily, oh so luckily, the defenders had been caught sleeping. Literally. Pilot Bob Bloomfield described seeing two Japanese pilots fastening their parachutes as they ran toward their planes—still wearing pajamas.

An estimated 80 enemy planes—Zeros, army fighters, and navy bombers—managed to get into the air. The faster, better-armored Hellcats feasted on them. At least 30 enemy planes were shot down—17 of them by *Intrepid* pilots. Ace Al Vraciu was credited with four of them. Numerous other aircraft were badly damaged and forced out of combat. By late afternoon, more than 250 Japanese planes had been destroyed—as many as 127 of them defeated in aerial dogfights.

With the defenders mostly wiped out, waves of bombers and torpedo planes began bombing and strafing the island. They owned the sky. The seaplane base was leveled; its 15 seaplanes were wrecked and sunk.

As each wave of returning raiders landed on *Intrepid*'s deck, reports of their success spread rapidly throughout the entire ship. Everyone was keeping score. They wanted to know what was happening out there. "First report we got was that our planes knocked down 8 Zeros and destroyed 3 Bettys on the ground," Montfort wrote. "The next group . . . sunk one torpedo boat, one large transport and set fire to one oiler besides starting large fires on the beach where many planes were caught napping. The next group was mainly T.B.F. [Grumman torpedo bombers] and the object was 43 cruisers, baby flattop and one destroyer. Of these we only got one torpedo hit on a cruiser . . . An observation plane reported the cruisers and destroyers had taken it on the lam."

Those enemy ships left in the lagoon were floating targets. At least 30 of them were sunk or badly damaged, including 2 light cruisers and 3 smaller cruisers, 4 destroyers, 2 submarine tenders, an armed fishing trawler, a troop carrier, tankers, and cargo ships. Several other ships tried to escape. They sailed into the waiting guns of the battleships *New Jersey* and *Iowa* and the heavy cruisers *Minneapolis* and *New Orleans*. They were battered.

Official reports estimated 200,000 tons of enemy shipping was destroyed—the most on any single day throughout the entire war. The official action report concluded, "The attack on Truk must certainly be accepted as a highly successful operation. A large tonnage of vitally important shipping, both combatant and supply, was destroyed or rendered inoperative for a long period; many of the enemy's dwindling aircraft were shot down or burned on the ground; the prestige of his leaders was gravely shaken at home . . ."

Intrepid had launched over 200 sorties. Air Group 6 sank 2 ships and crippled 10 more. Most of their crews came home. Most of them.

Intense Japanese antiaircraft fire knocked down or damaged 25 aircraft, among them 8 Hellcats. Fifteen fliers from *Intrepid* never returned to the ship. Lieutenant George Bullard was shot down and managed to swim to a nearby island; he alerted the squadron to his plight by writing "Bull—SOS" in the sand. A seaplane made a rescue attempt but failed to find him. The crew of a Japanese patrol boat landed and began searching for him. He managed to evade them for three days, but finally was captured, beaten, and imprisoned in a cell next to the heroic leader of the legendary Black Sheep Squadron, Pappy Boyington. Both men were transported to Japan, where they remained in prison until the end of the war.

Other airmen were not as fortunate. Avenger pilot Lieutenant Jim Bridges scored a direct hit on a Japanese freighter with four 500-pound bombs. That ship, it turned out, was hauling ammunition; its massive explosion threw debris more than a thousand feet into the air, riddling the dive-bomber. Bridges, tail gunner Robert Bruton, and turret gunner Jim Green were killed in action.

Lieutenant Paul Tepas died in a friendly fire incident when the *Iowa* mistakenly opened fire and shot him down.

Some air crews ditched their damaged planes and had to be rescued. It was tricky and dangerous—but necessary and effective. The Navy kept submarines on station during battles to rescue downed pilots. Battleships and cruisers carried seaplanes that were launched on catapults, then retrieved by a derrick after plucking downed pilots from the sea. When Essex' pilot George Blair had to ditch early in the morning, a seaplane was dispatched to pick him up. Blair climbed into the rear seat, sitting on the tail gunner's lap. But rather than immediately returning, the Kingfisher pilot spent the morning taxiing around the lagoon being directed—and protected—by Hellfire pilots as he picked up additional downed airmen. Eventually he rescued seven men; there was no room inside the fuselage, so some of them held on to the wings.

Obviously, he couldn't take off in that situation, so he taxied out of the lagoon and rendezvoused with a submarine, which took the rescued fliers aboard and eventually returned them to their carriers.

The attack on Truk had been more successful than anticipated. In the ensuing months, the loss of the atoll as a supply depot and air base would make it extremely difficult for the Japanese to defend other islands. "Uncle Sam's victory at Truk is a dream come true," the Associated Press reported days later, "for we have administered a defeat which has so rocked the Mikado's capital that the Japs are making no effort to conceal the devastating effects, both morale and material."

Japan's prime minister, General Hideki Tojo, responded to this defeat by firing his chiefs of staff for both the navy and army—and taking personal control of the army.

Task Force 58 ran dark and slow that night. Japanese submarines and planes were out there, searching for them. And they were desperate for retribution. Portholes were covered with blackout curtains; smoking was not permitted on deck. Radio communications were prohibited. The ships moved away from Truk at reduced speed, taking care not to leave a long wake the enemy could follow.

The carriers were nestled in the middle of smaller groups, protected by a screen of radar-equipped night fighters and destroyers.

The first bogey showed up on radar at 2111 hours. *Bogey* was military slang used to describe an unidentified and possibly hostile airplane; it was derived from the Middle English word *bugge*, meaning a frightening specter or a ghost. This ghost was a single aircraft. Based on its speed, it was presumed to be a twin-engine Betty, but it was impossible to make any kind of firm identification. Whatever it was, it was 21 miles away, flying at 1,500 feet. The Betty, actually a Mitsubishi G4M, was Japan's best land-based naval bomber, with a range of 2,300 miles. Earlier in the war, Bettys were credited with sinking the Royal Navy battleship HMS *Prince of Wales* and cruiser HMS *Repulse*. What made it especially dangerous was that in addition to bombs, a Betty could carry a single 800-kilogram Type 91 torpedo, the world's most accurate air-launched torpedo.

At times, this intruder dropped down to 500 feet, probably to get a better look at imagined shadows. It shot off several flares, but there was nothing to see. The plane was much too far away to be a threat to the carriers. In *Intrepid*'s CIC, Ray Stone and his team tracked the blip. He sipped his third cup of coffee as he watched the enemy pilot poking around. His course made it obvious he hadn't spotted anything that attracted his attention. He had just wandered into that area of the ocean. Good luck for him? Bad luck for the task force?

Sprague took no chances. He ordered *Intrepid* to general quarters. Gun crews slept in their tubs. Pilots sat in the cockpits of their fueled and armed night fighters. They waited, maintaining radio silence. The plane crossed their stern about 8 miles away, fading into the night.

Stone exhaled.

Twenty minutes later, the plane reappeared, now 33 miles away, but again disappeared.

A second *bandit*—this term was used to describe an aircraft confirmed to be hostile, and in this situation there was no doubt about that—was spotted minutes later, 40 miles from the task force but closing rapidly. It came within 5 miles and then suddenly veered away. Did it spot the carriers? Was it probing the defensive screen? Were more bombers en route?

It was going to be a long night.

There were eight men in the dimly lit command center, five "scope dopes" hunched over their screens, barely visible in the reflected green glow. Two men were on the radio telephones, one of them listening for any unexpected chatter, the other maintaining direct communications to the bridge. The eighth man was the spare, ready to fill in as needed.

They spoke radar. They had been trained to report calmly and clearly. There was no room for emotion, for fear or speculation. They reported what they saw on their screens. Nothing else. At 2257, one of them said loudly, "I've got three bogies northeast at 1,000 feet. Fourteen miles and closing."

Ray Stone checked his screen. There they were. Three white blips. One of the radiomen caught Ray's attention and tapped his wristwatch three times. It was eleven o'clock. Stone knew exactly what he meant: they had talked about it earlier, while waiting in the ready room to start their shift. It was only an hour before the end of the day, as if getting through the 16th safely would ensure their safety.

Stone had never paid much attention to that superstition. He frowned and shook his head. *Leave me alone with that stuff.*

"Five hundred feet. Northeast. Twelve miles. Still closing." Stone pursed his lips. Nothing to indicate they had spotted the task force. The waiting always was the hardest part; responding was easier. You just did what you were trained to do. At 10 miles away, two of them broke off, turned left, and began circling. The third bandit kept coming. Eight miles. Six miles. Four miles. It was within torpedo range when a cruiser screening the task force opened up on him. "Scared him off," Montfort wrote, "but not for long. The bogies knew where we were and returned, this time even closer . . . We couldn't see them, but we could hear them."

They came back. This time there were more of them. "They're out hunting for us," Jake Elefant remembered. "Came within 4 miles but very black and dark out they say. We sent up night fighters and all ships except carriers were firing."

The cruisers and battleships put up lethal walls of fire. Sustained ack-ack drove the Japanese back into the dark sky. One of the raiders was hit; it exploded in a spectacular fireball. The carriers remained silent, under orders to hold their fire so as not to reveal their positions. They were nestled in the middle of a defensive screen consisting of destroyers, cruisers, night fighters, and finally, battleships. They were the Holy Grail for the enemy and were to be protected at any cost.

Aboard *Intrepid*, the crew's jubilation at a job exceptionally well done that day was tempered by the reality that several members of their air group weren't coming home. The hours directly after a battle are emotionally exhausting as the adrenaline begins flowing out of your body. Most men have a need to talk about it. The airmen were relating every single minute of combat—the difficult air ballet, the close calls, the problems, the victories, and the questions about who saw a lost plane hit or going down: Did they see any chutes?

The crew boasted of their own feats: safely launching 200 flights, taking seconds off rearming and refueling planes to get them back in the air faster, supplying 3,000 hot meals and many gallons of coffee to men who stayed at their stations for hours. It had been a tremendous team effort. Everybody had a piece of this victory.

Meanwhile, the Japanese continued probing, crisscrossing the entire area.

Captain Sprague had kept the crew at general quarters through much of the day and into the night. It was a balancing act: readiness versus exhaustion. On the flight deck, men scanned the dark sky, but there was nothing to see. Whatever was happening was taking place miles away.

At 2345, with nothing showing on radar, Sprague finally decided to secure from general quarters. Take a deep breath. He set condition one easy, Navy lingo meaning, basically, the enemy was in the area and surprise contact was possible, so stay alert. "Key battle stations" were manned while "other personnel were at ease or allowed to sleep on station, rotating the personnel." The captain also ordered all hands to remain fully clothed, even in their bunks.

One easy also meant that the watertight doors, which had been closed, should be opened. Phil Reynolds ordered his damage control watch officers to take their positions near the opened doors.

Just in case.

No one slept well, if they slept at all. Those men who went back to their bunks kept their life vests and helmets inches away. They knew the enemy was hunting.

At 2349, radar detected a bandit almost 21 miles from the task force. It was designated Raid George. *Yorktown* sent up a night fighter to investigate, although his flight was controlled from *Enterprise*. He followed the raider for about 7 miles but did not make contact. The fighter was ordered to alter his course to bring him into a better position for radar guidance.

Minutes later, the bandit disappeared from radar screens. He was out there somewhere, flying just feet off the water, making it difficult to spot him. Where was he? Midnight. The second hand rolled smoothly into the next day, February 17. At 0004, Admiral Spruance signaled the task force to make an emergency left turn and increase speed to 25 knots.

The frantic search for the enemy invader continued. There was confusion between *Enterprise* and *Essex* over control of the friendly. At exactly midnight, 0000 hours, *Enterprise* ordered the night fighter to "break off" contact, fearing it might confuse antiaircraft fire. But the friendly complicated the situation by turning south, then west, remaining on radar screens.

Four minutes later, Captain Sprague ordered another sharp turn. This was exactly the type of emergency maneuvering *Intrepid* had practiced in its speed trials. He wasn't going to be a predictable target. The ship leaned hard to starboard; below, men braced themselves to maintain their balance.

Suddenly, *Intrepid* picked up the blip on its radar. "Jesus," Stone heard someone behind him say, a touch of alarm in his voice. "There he is. That fucker's heading right for us."

The bandit was behind the ship, heading directly towards it. Obviously he had spotted the ship's wake and was following it into the target. The plane was 300 yards abeam, off to the right side of the ship, flying at 50 feet.

On the bridge, there was considerable confusion. Was it a friendly? Maybe *Yorktown*'s night fighter? Its navigation lights were on, which provided some reassurance. An enemy plane would not make that mistake.

No one saw it drop the torpedo.

At 100 yards away, it rose sharply and flew right over the flight deck, so low that flight crewmen swore later they could have knocked it down with a rock. Aviation maintenance man Jerry Goguen said, "I could see the silhouettes of the pilot and radioman illuminated by the eerie green light from the plane's instrument panels."

Gunner Tony Zollo was in his bunk, wearing only his undershorts and socks. Zollo was part of the Marine detachment stationed aboard. He grabbed his pants and shoes, his vest and helmet, and started racing to his battle station on the hangar deck. Damage control was already locking down the ship: "The hatch was slammed closed just as I reach the ladder," Zollo remembered. *Okay*, he thought, *I can't get up to the deck that way*. "I turned and I am now at a run, going forward towards officer's country. I pass several ladders and hatches. They are shut. I finally find an open hatch . . . As I enter the island to go to my gun, I no longer have my shoes or my pants . . . I get to the gun. I grab a full ammo magazine as I pass through the ready room . . .

"As I looked to starboard I saw a twin-engined plane perhaps 500 yards off the ship's beam. The left engine of the plane is spitting red fire as though the engine is missing and not running smoothly. He then turned sharply left and flew across *Intrepid*'s flight deck—I don't believe the plane was higher than 35 feet above the flight deck as she passed over."

The plane was still visible when its torpedo smashed into the ship. The time was 0010, February 17. Seaman Ernest Faw and a friend had brought pillows on deck, intending to sleep under the stars. "There was a Marine on watch on the flight deck," Faw recalled. "All at once I heard him holler, 'He dropped it, he dropped it!' I raised up, and I could see the exhaust of this plane coming. It had two exhaust pipes, lit up like headlights. He was coming right at us. He went across the flight deck and was gunning it, getting out. But he had dropped a torpedo. I thought it was going to turn the ship over. The bow went down, and the stern went up, then it went down again."

Intrepid trembled; it shook as if an angry giant was rattling it. Within seconds, several compartments were flooded. The ship began listing to starboard.

Men were knocked off their feet; they bounced off bulkheads, fell off ladders, stumbled trying to retain their balance. For many crew members precisely what happened during the next few hours is hazy; memories were haphazard, shaped by necessity, fear, and injury. For the first time in their lives young men were confronted by the often grotesque damage of war and did whatever was necessary without pausing to think about it. Years later, these universal experiences became their individual memories.

Gordon Keith was lying restlessly in an upper bunk; he was lifted more than two feet into the air, his head smashing into the overhead as he was tossed onto the deck.

Frank Johnson was in his quarters, holding a winning hand in a penny-ante poker game as his coffee cooled. He was just laying down his cards when they got hit. The impact sent the cash and cards flying. The men were out of the room and on their way to their stations before the coins hit the ground.

On the flight deck, a crew member was thrown over the fan tail; he made a desperate grab for a steel cable, somehow incredibly managing to catch it. He literally held on for his life; hand over hand, he dragged himself back on board. His palms were ripped up and bloody, but he was alive.

There were a few seconds of general disbelief: *What the hell was that? Did we hit something? Again?*

Then reality took hold: the ship had been hit. *Intrepid* had been hit. In those first minutes, no one knew for certain what had hit them, just that it had done serious damage. Nor did they know if this was one torpedo, one bomb, one whatever. Whatever it was, it had done serious damage. The ship continued listing to starboard.

The entire ship erupted in choreographed chaos as men raced to their battle stations.

There was little panic. They had been training for this night, this minute, for so many months. The lessons of those endless, repetitive drills had turned hesitation into instinct. Men made instant life-and-death decisions. A group of chiefs were having coffee in the mess hall when the torpedo hit. The mess began flooding. They considered their options, then dived into the water and swam out. All of them survived.

All types of objects had been jarred loose from storage. Fire extinguishers were rolling free, hoses had unraveled, light fixtures were smashed, and fragments of shattered glass littered the passageways. On the flight deck, a skid holding a 1,000-pound bomb was sliding, forcing men to jump out of the way. A 1,000-pound bomb rolling on the deck? Nobody knew what would set it off. If it slid into an aircraft fuel line or crashed into a plane or a bulkhead the wrong way . . . There were no options. Five men got behind it and shoved it over the side.

Hatches were slammed closed while men were climbing the ladders. Watertight compartments were sealed. The fact that those doors had been opened only a few minutes earlier was pure luck. It was the difference between setting off a cherry bomb in a sealed can or an open one. Rather than containing and magnifying the energy of the explosion in several sealed compartments, blowing out the bulkheads, the force dissipated throughout the ship. Damage had been reduced significantly.

Not everyone responded well. A lieutenant panicked, running up and down the hangar deck yelling, "Prepare to abandon ship. Prepare to abandon ship."

Not every action that took place that night was recorded or made its way into official reports, but from the small mountain of memories and documents available it is probable this is how events unfolded: Captain Sprague took several deep breaths. He remained calm. He gave his orders in a firm but normal tone. That was vitally important. The crew would feed off his attitude. Phil Reynolds came onto the bridge. Wherever he had been, it was wet. His shirt was drenched. "How bad?" Sprague asked.

Reynolds shook his head. "Give me two minutes."

"Sound general quarters," Sprague ordered. Bells started clanging. "Steady as she goes," he told the helmsman. He had no intention of making any sudden or unexpected maneuvers. Not in the middle of a dark night. They'd ride this out. The memory of what had happened when *Indiana* made its surprising turn was still fresh. *Intrepid* would complete the turn.

The crew raced to their battle stations, some of them hindered by the blackout conditions. Phil Reynolds got on the speaker system. Keeping the men informed was essential. "We've taken a torpedo in the starboard quarter," he told them. Calmly. "Damage control parties, lay aft to your stations."

Damage control officers began reporting. Flooding. Smashed bulkheads. Sprague was trying to assess that information when the helmsman said, trying desperately to control the fear in his voice, the most terrifying words Sprague had heard in his long career: "Sir, she's not answering. We've lost steering."

For no logical reason the helmsmen held tight to the round wheel, as if he might unexpectedly regain control.

Sprague knew exactly what was going on. Damage control reported the torpedo had blasted into the steering room. It looked like it had taken out his steering mechanism. Damaged the rudder too, maybe even destroyed it.

But whatever the cause, the result was the same: *Intrepid* was out of control in the middle of the task force.

The reality was terrifying: 40,000 tons of steel, three football fields long, moving at 20 knots was running wild in a densely crowded, dark ocean. It was going to take all the luck the ship and all its men had in reserve to prevent a massive collision.

Sprague instantly ordered the starboard engines shut down. He had gamed variations of this scenario several times during his career. During the trials off New England, an outboard shaft had been locked down on one side while go-ahead full power was applied to the two shafts on the other side to figure out how to maintain a steady course. They'd spent a full day experimenting with different options, making adjustments, getting a feel for it. Sprague had enjoyed it; it was an inter- esting exercise, as he described it. A challenge.

But now? Now it was real. He was desperate. He was going to try to use his engines to regain some control. It could work, assuming the propellers had not been damaged. They would find that out in a few seconds.

He got on the speaker to alert the crew. "This is your Captain speaking," he said matter-of-factly. There was no fear, no panic in his voice. *Stay calm. We'll handle this. A walk in the park.* "Men, we have been torpedoed. The ship's rudder is jammed, and we are turning east through the task force. Stand by for a possible collision."

A possible collision? At this speed? Jesus. Jesus H. Christ. A collision? There must be something the captain could do prevent it. There just had to be. Ships didn't crash in the . . . The memory of the *Indiana* and *Washington* popped into a lot of minds. A night just like this one. Ten men had been killed, but compared to this?

The potential consequences were almost unimaginable. Almost all of them found something bolted down, grabbed hold tightly, and took a long, deep breath. Many others closed their eyes and prayed. And waited. And waited.

With the task force running black, it was impossible to see more than a hundred yards in any direction. That didn't matter. Everybody knew that the largest task force of the war, more than 100 ships were somewhere out there in the darkness. Sprague had broken radio silence to warn the fleet that he had lost control of his ship, there was nothing they could do to avoid a collision. It takes time—too much time—to maneuver a warship, even when you know what is coming towards you. But *Intrepid* had no path. It was out of control, impossible to track.

As damage control fought to save the ship, Sprague was trying everything he could conjure to regain control. He had been in tight spots before; on two different occasions, the engine of his plane had failed. He had seconds to save his life. He'd figured it out, got it restarted. He'd lost his landing gear once and made a perfect belly landing. He'd been in typhoons that spun his ship around, that literally covered it with a rogue wave and almost capsized it. But this? Running amok through the entire task force without any controls?

For those few minutes, *Intrepid* was little more than a pinball careening through a sea of massive moving bumpers.

And then, out of the night, a dark shadow took form. The *Essex*. On *Intrepid*'s deck, men stood transfixed. They were on a collision path. There was nothing they could do to avoid it.

Aboard *Essex*, Captain Ralph Ofstie sounded general quarters. He changed his speed and course, trying desperately to avoid impact. Ofstie and Tom Sprague had known each other since their days at the academy, where Ofstie had been a year behind him. They'd gone through flight school at Pensacola together and been early supporters of the carrier concept.

But all of their combined training, the decades of experience under challenging conditions, none of it mattered. There was literally nothing they could do to change fate.

On *Intrepid*, Sprague was desperately working his engines, shutting down the port engines, giving full power to his starboard engines, trying to turn away. On *Essex*, the equally cool Ofstie had ordered an emergency turn, trying to get out of the way.

Luck.

That's all it was. Wonderful, beautiful luck. In the end, it was luck that determined the outcome. The luck of the 17th. *Essex* glided past *Intrepid*'s fantail, yards apart, two ships passing safely in the night. *Intrepid* cut right through *Essex*'s wake.

Sprague cleared his throat, swallowed, and said to no one in particular, "Well, that was interesting."

As *Essex* faded into the darkness, Sprague continued struggling to bring *Intrepid* under control. There still were other ships out there, a lot of them, most of them scrambling to get as far away from *Intrepid* as possible.

It gradually became apparent that he could keep at least a minimal degree of control by using the engines as thrusters: one at full power while the other one was shut down, then reverse it, back and forth. The result was a zigzag course, but it allowed Sprague to "steer" his ship.

While this was going on, the crew fought to seal the leaks and immediately began rescue operations—if there was anyone to rescue. Throughout the ship, men were risking their lives to perform heroic deeds. Everybody was banged up, some bones had been broken, but men with minor injuries ignored them to assist the more severely injured.

Making the situation even more difficult, and dangerous, was the fact that the ship was running dark, lit only by dim red lighting. Fallen and scattered debris made it difficult and dangerous to move too fast or too far. The open hangar deck was completely blacked out and enveloped by rising smoke, making it nearly impossible for men to see even a few feet in front of them. Several members of damage control teams were injured when they tripped over ropes or cables or ran into parked planes while rushing to their stations.

While the ship was still running wild through the task force, parachute riggers Perry Carroll Jr. and Ed Houde, who had been working on the flight deck when the ship was hit, heard loud screams for help. But they couldn't figure out where they were coming from. They finally found the source. Three men were trapped on a catwalk that had come loose on the side of the ship. They were stunned. The gun tub that had been there was gone, blown away. The catwalk leading to that tub was all that was left, hanging precariously off the side of the ship. Two of the men were lying on their backs. The third man was sitting up. They were all injured. There was no way of knowing how badly they were hurt.

The catwalk was about 15 feet below the flight deck; it was banging against the hull. There was no easy way to get to them. With the assistance of several other crewmen, Carroll and Houde tied ropes around their waists and under their arms, then dropped over the aft end of the flight deck. They lowered themselves down into the mangled steel hull, as if descending a jagged steel mountain, finally reaching a narrow, unprotected ledge. They got their footing, then moved cautiously through the wreckage until they reached the catwalk. Using ropes, the men on deck managed to lift their wounded crewmates to safety.

Two dive-bombers tied down on the flight deck had been ripped loose by the explosion and careened into the radar mast, causing it to collapse; numerous heavy pieces were left swaying above the deck. Several of them were banging against the mast, threatening to bring the whole structure down. Lieutenant Paul Combs and Chief Radioman Bobby Warren gingerly climbed 30 feet up the mast, like young lads clambering up the yardarm of a sailing ship. They secured the broken parts to prevent further damage.

Chief Machinist's Mate Jim Nesmith and Chief Electrician's Mate Gerry Hill were in their bunks on the third deck when the torpedo ripped into the hull. Like most of the men in their compartment, they were thrown into the bulkheads, then slammed down hard on the deck. They were dazed and bleeding.

Within seconds, the ocean began seeping in.

Rather than scrambling out to ensure their own safety, Nesmith and Hill stayed behind. Nesmith physically prevented several confused chief petty officers from trying to escape through an area now open to the sea, which might well have proved a fatal mistake. Meanwhile Hill, using a hand lantern, calmly led several dazed and injured crewmates through dark corridors as they filled with rising waters until they reached a ladder to the upper deck.

No one knew how many men had been killed. Rumors spread quickly. Supposedly several crew members had been tossed over the side and were lost. At least one gun tub had been ripped off the side of the ship. Other men had been trapped in flooding compartments.

Life-and-death decisions had been made. As the ocean flooded the steering gear room, its watertight doors had been sealed with several men trapped inside. While the odds were against them, there was a slim possibility some of them were still alive. There was always hope. It wasn't impossible. But the only way to find out was to have someone dive in there. Chief Mechanic Tom Rock and machinist George Schlemmer volunteered. Schlemmer was familiar with the layout of the room, having previously installed an emergency hand pump that led to the ram room, where the rudder was located.

Neither man had any diving experience. They put on shallow water diving equipment, basically a gas mask that the Navy had converted for exactly this kind of emergency situation. The mask provided only a few minutes of oxygen, but that would be sufficient to search for survivors. If they were there, they would find them.

Rock and Schlemmer stripped to their underwear. Ropes were tied around both men's waists to ensure they would be able to find their way out. They carried waterproof flashlights that allowed them to see about two feet in front of them in the swirling water. The two men descended into the flooded compartment.

The room was pitch-black and Pacific-cold. They would not be able to stay there for more than a few minutes. They moved slowly, feeling their way around the room—until Schlemmer walked into the first floating body.

They recovered three bodies: Robert Stallins, Bill Lear, and Al Moscaritolo. They tied a rope around each of them and pulled them out of the compartment. They saw at least two more, but twisted metal prevented them from reaching them. Then they made a quick inspection of the damage so they could report it.

The compartment was open to the sea.

It was time to get out. They were running low on oxygen. But Schlemmer had an outrageous idea. The 34-year-old Navy vet from Custer, Oklahoma, wanted to lower himself into the ram room and use a hand pump to try to center the rudder. It was a bold and daring plan—that had an extremely limited chance of success. Whatever damage had been done to the rudder had required incredible force. It was a huge piece of curved metal, and one man working alone underwater would not be able to rectify it.

Almost certainly it was a suicide mission—the room had been ripped open by the torpedo—but he volunteered to make the attempt. Before he could do it, Lieutenant Commander Tom Wallace, the assistant damage control officer, ordered him out of the compartment. Enough men had been lost, he knew, there was nothing more that could be done.

Intrepid had been struck a heavy blow. The ship was wounded. No one yet knew how severely. Its crew responded with bravery and determination. Those men who could be saved had been saved. By sealing watertight compartments, the flooding had been contained, although the ship continued to list.

It was obvious the ship was out of the fight. It could not stay with the task force. Admiral Montgomery ordered the destroyers *Owen*, *Stephen Potter*, and *The Sullivans* to drop back to protect *Intrepid* from enemy poachers.

Meanwhile, section chiefs began checking on their men, trying to determine how many of them were wounded or missing. The count grew through the night.

As Elefant reported in his diary, "At about 1:30 the exec congratulated us on how calmly we took it all and at the same time the moon rose fully. We thought sure as hell we were goners as the bogies were still on the screen looking for us. Stayed at G.Q. all night and somehow luck was with us as they didn't find us . . .

"Morning came and were we glad to see the sunrise."

Luck.

FIVE

Mr. and Mrs. Emilio Moscaritolo
14 Davenport Street
Haverhill, Massachusetts

Dear Mr. and Mrs. Moscaritolo,

The officers and men join me in expressing our sympathy in the death of your son, Alphonse Vincent Moscaritolo, Seaman, First Class. He was a loyal and cheerful shipmate, and his passing well deserves a sacred remembrance among the heroes of our Country.

His death resulted from enemy action, and burial was held at sea on February 18, 1944.

The Catholic Chaplain presided at the services in which religious and military honors were paid his memory. May God grant you comfort in your sorrow.

Respectfully yours,
T. L. Sprague
Captain, U.S. Navy
Commanding

THE TOLL WAS devastating: 9 men had been killed in the attack, 9 others were seriously wounded; 2 of those men would die, and another 28 suffered injuries severe enough to send them to the sick bay. At least 6 men were unaccounted for but eventually would be found safe. The ship itself had suffered significant damage, although in those first few hours, it was impossible to determine the full extent of it or the immediate consequences other than the loss of steering. That would come in the following days.

While throughout the ship, individual acts of heroism were taking place, on the bridge, Captain Sprague was calmly imposing order, instituting standard procedures that had been put in place to deal with combat damage situations. Tom Sprague had been training for this night from his first days at Annapolis. One of his first fitness reports, submitted by the commander of the Naval Air Station at Pensacola, described his temperament as "calm, forceful, active." And noted that his "Physical and nervous endurance under strain" were "Excellent!"

While Sprague was assigned as a structural and engineering officer in San Diego, his commander had praised his ability to "recognize and solve difficult technical problems . . . with outstanding results" and added he was "skillful and experienced in handling men. Unusually well-suited for command."

A standard fitness report prepared by Admiral Henry Mullinnix just before Sprague assumed command of *Intrepid* addressed his "Reactions in emergencies: With reference to the faculty of acting instinctively in a logical manner in difficult and unforeseen situations." The admiral rated him "Exceptionally cool-headed and logical in his actions under all conditions."

The next few days would test that.

At different stations throughout his career, he had studied engine design and performance, structural engineering, and the properties of fire. He had been taught the principles of leadership and problem-solving. In his more than two decades in the service, he had compiled a vast storehouse of information and experience that he was able to instantly access.

Equally important, perhaps even more important, was his natural ability to inspire confidence in his crew. In a combat zone, with a damaged and vulnerable ship, that made a difference. They felt strongly that their captain knew what he was doing, that he was able to balance their welfare with the needs of the ship, and they could rely on his judgment.

The crew had responded magnificently. Those days and weeks and months of boring, repetitive damage control training had paid off. Go here, do this, close that door, turn that switch, carry this equipment, don't touch that; now do it again. And again. It had all paid off. Procedures that had been developed and instituted over the previous decades had been put into real-time practice to limit injuries and halt the spread of life-threatening conditions like fire, smoke, dangerous debris, and gas leaks. Very few men had been injured after the initial explosion.

That was not luck. In the years between World Wars, the Navy had focused on developing the mundane skills of damage control. It had spent decades and millions of dollars to answer one question: How do we keep a damaged ship afloat and fighting?

The answers to that question had been built into the *Essex*-class carriers or were later incorporated in fittings and had proved their value. These ships were designed with more compartments both below and above the waterline. Isolation valves allowing sailors to shut down damaged systems while others could continue functioning were placed throughout ships, and in addition to handheld extinguishers, numerous fire plugs were installed so that at least two 100-foot hoses from different plugs could reach any point on the ship.

This mammoth effort paid off when *Intrepid* got hit.

Most civilians knew nothing about the emphasis the Navy had placed on damage control. Sailors knew it, though. It had been drilled into them from their first day in boot camp. "Damage control will be with you every minute of your life that is spent on board ships," Captain Thomas J. Kelly had written in his essential primer, *Damage Control*. "From the instant you step over the main deck beading of your first ship, Damage Control is vital to your existence . . . Every officer and man on board ship has a duty to perform in Damage Control . . ."

The stated objective of damage control was simple: keep the ship in condition to fight. That means, Kelly wrote, "preserving the watertight integrity, maneuverability and stability of the vessel." Doing that begins with three steps:

1. The damage must be localized and limited to prevent the spreading of fire, water, or gas to other parts of the ship.

2. The full extent of the damage must be determined, and a decision made as to what can be done to counter the damage suffered.

3. The steps necessary and possible must be undertaken
   and completed at the earliest possible moment.

The Germans, Kelly wrote, were the first to place importance
on it: "Their ships were carefully designed and constructed with
the utmost care." The study of damage control had begun in
1897 when Kaiser Wilhelm ordered Secretary of the Imperial
Navy Admiral Alfred von Tirpitz to build a fleet of warships
capable of challenging Britain's domination of the seas.

The biggest threat to a ship was an explosion below the
waterline; that's what made torpedoes and mines so dangerous. Throughout history, a single explosion at or below the
waterline often had been enough to sink a ship. Once the hull
was breached, the ocean would be relentless, exploiting every small opening to flow through the ship and drag it down.
The result of von Tirpitz's experiments was the concept of
creating watertight compartments within a single hull. Constructing ships with numerous compartments that could be
isolated made moving around the ship less convenient, but it
allowed damage to be contained.

Watertight compartments might have saved *Intrepid*. The
Japanese torpedo had struck the ship 15 feet below the waterline. It had opened the ship to the Pacific like a tin can. It
was literally possible to look at the damage from above and
see through the ship into the ocean. But the flooding had
been limited to several sealed compartments. The ship listed
4 degrees, but while that created some anxiety, it was never
in danger of sinking.

While the concept of designing ships with numerous
watertight compartments was relatively new to the West, the

Chinese had been incorporating it in their ships for almost a thousand years. von Tirpitz probably had borrowed his design concept from the earliest Chinese shipbuilders.

As early as 1405, decades before Columbus set sail, a 317-ship fleet carrying 28,000 sailors commanded by Admiral Zheng He made 7 voyages to establish diplomatic and trade relationships throughout Southeast Asia and East Africa.

Admiral He's fleet was led by mammoth 3,000-ton, 9-masted multidecked warships. They each were 400 feet long and 170 feet wide with a 50,000-square-foot deck large enough to hold Columbus's entire fleet. These ships were built with the hull divided into numerous watertight compartments, enabling the fleet to carry a monthslong supply of fresh drinking water and other supplies—as well as survive damage below the waterline.

But it would be centuries before Tirpitz proved to the West in the World War I battles of Dogger Bank and Jutland that watertight compartments were essential. German warships were battered by the British fleet but continued fighting and were quickly and easily repaired. In 1918's Battle of Imbros, for example, the German battlecruiser *Goeben* was struck by three British mines but stayed afloat and successfully reached port, while the dreadnought HMS *Audacious*—which lacked sealed compartments—struck a single German mine in the Irish Sea, flooded slowly, and sank.

As a comparison, *Titanic* had 16 watertight compartments on its lowest level—a revolutionary design feature that supposedly made the ship unsinkable. But these compartments were only watertight horizontally. When the ocean filled a compartment, it could flow over the top of the wall into an adjoining compartment. Six of those compartments were breached, causing the ship to flood at its bow, which pulled *Titanic* under. The *Essex*-class carriers, including *Intrepid*, by comparison, had 750 watertight compartments, making them extraordinarily difficult to sink.

The ability of the German fleet to survive and continue fighting after sustaining major damage had surprised and greatly impressed American Navy leaders. After the Great War, a copy of the Imperial German Navy's damage control regulations was translated, and copies were circulated throughout the fleet. Navy boards recommended increasing the number of watertight compartments and instituting regular training for all sailors to control damage. Tirpitz's essential message that effective damage control can determine the outcome of a battle was adopted by the United States.

By the mid-1930s, the Navy was determined to implement reliable damage control procedures. A 1936 article in *U.S. Naval Institute Proceedings* reported that damage control had become haphazard, that the sailors running it aboard ships were "a motley assortment of ship fitters, carpenter's mates, electricians, various engineering ratings and whatever other ratings might be included in repair parties." While those sailors were capable of dealing with issues within their assigned specialty, they lacked the expertise to deal with issues outside that area.

A more systematic approach was needed. The article suggested that a specialized rating, damage control officer, be created, and that this officer should be trained in all aspects of emergency measures to limit casualties, make repairs, and maintain necessary equipment. It recommended a school should be opened in a ship environment to facilitate that training.

The Navy instituted each of these suggestions. It established the Naval Damage Control Training School in Philadelphia, which published its own 510-page handbook.

The job of damage control officer was loosely defined by Thomas Kelly: "The Damage Control Officer should know more about the ship than any other officer or man on board. He will be the first officer up in the morning and the last one to turn in at night . . . By his understanding of the ship, its structure and the organization and ability of each individual division he can be of outstanding assistance to the Captain and Executive Officer . . .

"His work is never done—there will always be something that he could do that will improve the ship's ability to perform her mission." And he might have been describing *Intrepid*'s damage control officer, Phil Reynolds, when he added, "With all of the above his ability to smile, give instructions and be patient will be invaluable to a combatant vessel operating under the strain of war conditions."

Ironically, the Japanese success at Pearl Harbor became an incubator for significant changes that played a role in their eventual defeat. Most of the ships sunk or damaged in the attack were designed and built incorporating then state-of-the-art damage control standards. They had been attacked with the bombs and torpedoes the Japanese would use throughout the war. Fortunately, rather than being sunk in the depths of the ocean, many of them had settled on the shallow bottom of the harbor. The majority of those ships would be raised, repaired, and returned to fight in the war.

But while the fleet was still burning, Navy investigators began inspecting each ship to find out what had worked to limit damage—and what had failed. They learned how design and structural elements had responded to enemy fire, how progressive flooding had caused the loss of stability, where more or stronger bolts might be needed, which hatches and pipes bent or broke, how the sprinkler systems performed, where fire hoses should be located, how many portable pumps were needed, and in every case, what had caused a ship to remain afloat—even after being hit multiple times—while others had sunk or capsized.

Second to flooding, fire proved to be the greatest threat to a ship's survival. Fires killed men, destroyed equipment, prevented repairs from being made, and could eventually gut the ship. After the Battle of Jutland, for example, British ships reported that sailors had been prevented from fighting fires by molten lead dripping from wires and by flames and smoke rising from linoleum decking and other combustible materials. So for more than a decade, the Navy had been systematically removing and replacing flammable materials.

Four American carriers had been lost early in the months after Pearl Harbor; three of them, the *Wasp*, *Hornet*, and *Lexington*, had to be abandoned and eventually were sunk because fires could not be contained. Only *Yorktown* had been lost to flooding.

In response, the Navy stripped warships of anything that might burn, including rubber sheeting, cork insulation, linoleum, certain types of canvas and cloth, and even paint. Paint in particular was problematic, as it was necessary to prevent corrosion and rust, but when exposed to high temperatures, some paints released dangerous gases. Where possible, paint was stripped before going into battle or replaced with less dangerous latex or water-based paints.

The new *Essex*-class carriers had incorporated all of these lessons in their design and fittings, but *Intrepid*'s survival just after midnight on February 17 came down to the response of the crew and the effectiveness of their training.

Within seconds of the explosion, Phil Reynolds and Assistant Damage Control Officer Tom Wallace raced to the damage control station on the island. This was Reynolds's first combat experience as the damage control officer. He had been recommended for the job by his commander while serving as an instructor in marine engineering at Annapolis: "Lt. Cmdr Reynolds is conscientious and thorough in the performance of his duty. Would make an excellent Damage Control and Engineering Officer of a capital ship."

Only 10 months later, he was getting his first test under enemy fire.

All that was known in those first few minutes after the attack was that the ship had been hit somewhere and suffered severe damage. Wallace immediately began getting information from "phone talkers," men trained to report damage at their stations. The phones were working. Reports started coming in.

Seconds after the torpedo hit his ship, Captain Sprague ordered, "All hands man your battle stations." This was a moment he had been waiting for, preparing for, since 1917. Like his peers, he had brushed against World War I without seeing action. Since then, he had studied war. He learned the history. He saw the films and read the books. He talked about it, wondered about it, and practiced for it. But the attack on Truk had been his first combat experience—although even that was limited to servicing the planes and pilots who did the real job. There had been danger, but no contact with the enemy.

Now his ship was under attack.

His response was bred in his bones. Tom Sprague never talked about it, but he could trace his lineage back to England and then the American colonies, back at least to Admiral Sir Edward Spragge, a former pirate who had been knighted by Charles II in 1665 for his gallantry in combat against the Dutch. The family coat of arms featured a demilion with a naval crown, a symbol usually awarded to a man who first boarded an enemy ship. Edward Spragge was, legendary English diarist Samuel Pepys wrote, personable and popular among his men, "A merry man who sang a pleasant song pleasantly."

Other ancestors had sailed from Dorsetshire in 1628 and settled in the Massachusetts Bay colony. There were Spragues at the Boston Tea Party, Spragues who fought and were wounded in the Revolutionary War, Spragues in the Spanish-American War. Three Spragues had served this country as senators. Two of them had been governor of Rhode Island. Several more had been members of congress and judges and renowned poets and artists. Naturalist Isaac Sprague had been with John Jay Audubon on his fabled expedition up the Missouri River.

One distant relative, the one he most closely resembled, Frank Sprague, had graduated from Annapolis in 1874 and eventually gained fame as an inventor for his work with electric motors. Frank Sprague had worked closely with Thomas Edison for a time, then had made significant contributions on his own to the development of the electric motor, electric railways, and electric elevators, making an impact on the development of modern cities. Perhaps coincidently, motors were also Tom Sprague's area of expertise; he'd even supervised the Navy's Aeronautical Engine Laboratory for a year.

And then there was his sister Norah, who danced in the spotlights of the Ziegfeld Follies.

Now it was time for Tom Lamison Sprague to add his name to his illustrious family's history. The fate of one of the greatest warships ever built and the more than 3,000 men who sailed her was in his hands.

Intrepid began listing at its stern. While Sprague was fighting to regain control of the ship, Reynolds and Wallace were directing damage control operations. They ordered the ship to "Condition Zed," all hatches were sealed, and they began counterflooding to keep the ship balanced and prevent it from capsizing.

Within minutes, crewmen began reporting damage. Water was flowing into several compartments. Chemical fumes were detected in one area. The source could not be immediately identified. Gasoline from ruptured plane tanks on the flight deck was leaking into the hangar deck. Casualties were being transported to sick bay.

Initial reports described the direct damage from impact as a "hole in the fourth deck approximately 20' x 30'" in the aft steering room, "although the bulkhead appeared to be holding." Reynolds directed that all available submersible pumps be taken there to begin pumping. Sprague asked, "Can you get some people into the aft steering room so we know exactly what's going on?"

Reynolds had told Frank Johnson to get down there, and Johnson was making his way through the debris of the ship to inspect the damage. If anyone could answer that question, it was Johnson. "We'll know pretty soon," he said.

The rupture extended vertically all the way up to the hangar deck, creating a small hole in that deck.

The gasoline leak was caused by two Douglas Dauntless dive-bombers that had been blown over the side. The volatile gasoline was being hosed off. The two bombers that had smashed into the radar mast had been badly damaged. They would have to be pushed into the Pacific.

A minute later, the fire alarm went off in the dope stowage and acid locker; potentially deadly fumes were being released. Wallace sent men to check it.

At 0016, roughly 10 minutes after being hit, men at the site reported to Reynolds that the steering gear was completely out "and the rudder jammed left about 15 degrees." The details were ominous: the rudder had been badly bent, the rudder post casting was broken—obviously it could not be repaired. *Intrepid* could not be steered from the helm.

Reports kept coming into damage control, always calmly. Numerous pipes, electrical cables, oil cables, and gasoline lines had been broken or ruptured. Doors and bulkheads had been damaged, and several of them were buckling. Life rafts and life nets were blown overboard.

A smoke bomb on the fantail had been ruptured; it was emitting a trail of smoke, leaking gases and acid. Wallace dispatched a team to the site, "and make sure you got your masks and breathers." It took them several minutes to get there because open ammunition boxes were blocking passageways. When they finally managed to get to the bomb, repeated attempts to stop the leak failed. They tried to jettison the bomb, but that too failed—the chute used to jettison bombs could not be opened without certain tools, and they couldn't find those tools in the debris because they had no light. A final attempt to physically move the smoke bomb also failed. It was much too heavy. There was no time to deal with it. There was too much else to do. The locker was sealed.

Chief Boatswain's Mate Frank Johnson was making his way down to the bowels of the ship, continually assessing and reporting the extent of the damage to Reynolds.

Johnson was one of those knowledgeable, reliable, dependable, respected men who made a big ship work. The young sailors in the crew listened to veterans like Johnson, followed his lead, and learned from him. But so did the "90-day wonders," the junior officers who had received only three months of training before being shipped out to fill a desperate need. During his 24 years in the Navy, Frank Johnson had served on more than a dozen ships, under numerous commanders and officers; he could tell the cut of a man's jib in three sentences. Officers didn't intimidate him. He also knew how to navigate the rules and regulations, having bumped up against them several times in his career.

Few men aboard *Intrepid* knew the ship as well as him. He also had a size advantage; at 5 feet 3 inches, he was small enough to fit through narrow openings in the damage. He had finally reached the aft steering room and was trying to determine the extent of the damage to the steering assembly and the rudder without getting in the way of the men trying to check for survivors or recover the bodies.

There wasn't much that could be done. "It's a God damn mess," he told Reynolds. In the few months they had been working together, Reynolds and Johnson had developed a strong relationship. They were real career Navy; unlike these young sailors, they had been there before the war and would be there—keeping the Navy running—when it was all over. In fact, only a month earlier, Reynolds had recommended to Captain Sprague that Johnson be promoted to chief. So Reynolds knew that he could rely on Johnson's assessment—and his candor. "I can't get in there," he said. "But from what I can see we're f-ed. There's f-ing crap all over the f-ing place, Sir. It's flooded. There's no way of getting in there."

As they spoke, Johnson heard the buzz of other people in the background reporting to damage control. And, he imagined, he could also hear Reynolds's mind absorbing the information. "Okay, Chief, see what else you got going on down there."

Then he clicked off. Johnson continued moving through the lower decks. He'd been in some scrapes during his career. While on the destroyer *Ludlow* two years earlier, a rogue wave had swept him off his feet and carried him down the deck. He'd been pretty badly banged up, really screwed up his elbow, but this was the first time he'd been torpedoed.

The amount of damage surprised him; that one explosion had put tremendous stress on bolts and joints and equipment far away from the point of impact. You never knew how deadly the aftereffects of an explosion could be. Johnson had lost friends on *Lexington*. He wasn't about to ignore that lesson.

The Lady Lex had been hit by both dive-bombers and torpedo planes in the Coral Sea. She was badly damaged but had survived the initial attacks. The watertight seals had contained the flooding and kept her afloat. It looked like she would be okay. But aircraft fuel lines that hadn't been properly drained created a volatile mixture of air and aviation fuel. Something sparked, the fumes ignited, fires blazed out of control. The crew had been forced to abandon her.

Lexington had been destroyed by secondary damage. Had those fuel lines been purged, she might have been saved. Because of that, procedures had been expanded. Even places that appeared to have suffered only minor or even no damage had to be inspected.

Johnson and several other veterans went methodically through the ship, searching for possible problems. The makeshift still in the crew quarters, for example, had been untouched, while the chief petty officers' mess had taken a beating. Tables and chairs had been thrown around, a portion of the bulkhead ceiling had collapsed, and there was more than two feet of water in the compartment. Using a flashlight, Johnson put on boots and managed to squeeze between upturned and damaged furniture to inspect the bulkheads. It was a tight fit in places—a submerged coffeepot surprised him and snared his foot—but he shook it off and continued his inspection. He found some minor wrinkles in a bulkhead, and the watertight door was slightly out of line. That was how the water had gotten in. Otherwise there was no danger. Soon as they got some light in there, the mess could be restored. Probably not the coffeepot, though. That had been dented when he kicked it across the room.

Electrical shorts were a big worry. Power had been blown or shut off in various parts of the ship. Before it could be restored, Dick Montfort and his crew had to make sure there were no exposed wires or other fire hazards. Montfort had been working for Consolidated Edison during the terrifying Long Island Express, the 1938 hurricane that had devastated the island, and had spent weeks afterwards inspecting and repairing generators. Compromising safety was not part of his personality. He was painstakingly thorough. No one was going to get hurt on his watch. "It'll be ready when it's ready," he replied testily when Reynolds tried to push him. While that sometimes made him difficult work with, it also meant his word was gold. Either he or one of his men went through every accessible compartment, and only after they were satisfied there was no danger would they sign off on it.

As soon as one problem was resolved, it seemed like two more popped up. Deck plates had buckled in several compartments. If they collapsed, it could cause a chain reaction. Repair crews were shoring them up as well as possible, but they couldn't guarantee it would hold. Maybe, probably, hopefully was the best answer they could give. Wallace made sure there was a man at each stress point; if it buckled, he needed to know immediately.

Reynolds remained standing on the bridge as he fought for the ship, walking around the room, sometimes pausing to stretch. Working that way kept him on his toes—literally and figuratively. At times in his career, he had gone hours without sitting down. In this situation, he lost all awareness of time, except that there wasn't enough of it. As each station reported, he pictured it in his mind, made notes, and at least

some of the time could visualize the damage. He had prepared for it. He had been there, wherever "there" was. He
had seen it, explored it, learned how it worked, and, in most
cases, knew the men reporting.

At 0142, the immediate threats to the ship resolved, Repair Crew VII "reported the loss of No. 15 20MM gun tub
on starboard side aft."

Reynolds took the information without showing any emotion. That was his job. "Loss?" Some part of him wanted to
ask that the information be repeated, just to be certain. But
he knew what "loss" meant. The tub had gone into the sea.
Men had gone with it. Normally there were at least four or
five men there. Sometimes more. There was no mention of
survivors.

There was nothing to be done. And no time to dwell on
it. He and Wallace continued responding to the information they were getting. Send a repair crew there. Close these
valves, open those valves. Bring pumps there. Rig auxiliary
electrical outlets. Open this hatch to vent smoke. Reynolds
made every decision in a firm, clear voice so there would no
confusion or hesitation. *Do it now.*

They were juggling dozens of situations. The crew in the
aft steering room had finally gotten the water pumps working: "A slight gain on water was reported." The smoke bomb
finally had been safely removed from the fantail without any
casualties. Homer Fox, a ship's carpenter, had figured out that
the fumes in the dope stowage and acid locker were coming
from smashed acid carboys, large glass containers. He described
them as "sweet-smelling, very heavy and dense, resembling a
white fog and very difficult to breathe and burning to the eyes."

And potentially very dangerous. Repair Team I opened several hatches to begin venting the fumes.

Reynolds glanced at his watch. More than two hours had passed since they had been hit. The ship had been stabilized. It was safe enough to open several hatches and doors to the mess halls so the men could get fresh water. Ventilation valves were also opened. The bake shop was opened.

By 0400, three bodies had been recovered from the aft steering room. There were no further reports on gun tub #15.

No one aboard the ship slept that night. New problems kept popping up. A sailor trying to release a jammed elevator guard rail had accidently ruptured a Hellcat's gas tank. Once again gasoline dripped down on the hangar deck and into the elevator pit, leaving them one spark from disaster. Firefighting crews hosed down the area.

At 0600, as the first light of the day brightened the horizon, an 18-inch triangular rip was discovered on the starboard side, flooding at least one compartment to the waterline.

By 0800, only small puddles of water were left on deck, although several compartments remained flooded. There was no way of making any repairs on the steering mechanism at sea, but all possible steps had been taken to prevent further damage. Ballast tanks had been pumped to compensate for the list. Captain Sprague ordered the ship secured from general quarters.

There was one last request made to the crew. Six volunteers in clean dungarees were to report to Johnson. Pallbearers were needed.

The practice of burying sailors at sea can be traced back through history to the Greeks, Romans, and Egyptians—but more as a matter of necessity than tradition. In fact, when a port was within a day's sail, the deceased most often was buried on land. Even Viking funerals, in which a ship was burned, were frequently held on land. Only when longer voyages made it impossible to preserve a body were men given to the ocean.

Those ancient civilizations supposedly believed that sea birds would carry the remains of the deceased into heaven, and by honoring their shipmates, they protected the ship from evil.

It was not recorded when the first American sailor was buried at sea. There is no more solemn ceremony in the Navy than honoring a departed shipmate. Sailmaker Gordon Keith and two assistants worked through the night and into the morning sewing the five canvas shrouds. This was the most unpleasant but necessary part of Keith's job. Long after ships no longer needed sails to be sewn or repaired, the sailmaker rating remained, perhaps because it was a far less ominous description than "undertaker." Herman Melville had written about the sailmaker in his novel *White Jacket*: "Just before daybreak, two of the sail-maker's gang drew near, each with a lantern, carrying some canvas, two large shot, needles, and twine. I knew their errand; for on men-of-war the sail-maker is the undertaker.

"They laid the body on deck, and, after fitting the canvas to it, seated themselves, cross-legged like tailors, one on each side, and, with their lanterns before them, went to stitching away, as if mending an old sail."

The Royal Navy traditionally wrapped a sailor in his hammock, sometimes with all his clothing or belongings and a five-pound shot to weigh them down, but Keith cut the proper lengths from the bolts of canvas the ship carried. He did all the sewing himself. As he did, he forced himself to think about his life at home, in Milo. About the good times, days at the lake, the football games, anything but the job he was doing. He didn't know any of the men personally, least he was pretty sure he didn't; their names weren't familiar, and he didn't look at their remains. He was very careful about each stitch, though. These were his crewmates, and he owed them that.

At 1100 hours on February 19, those men not on duty gathered on the hangar deck. While several pilots had been killed, the air group was kind of a separate entity; these were the first crew members to be killed in an enemy attack. Three of them had drowned when the aft assembly room flooded. Two of them were chief petty officers enjoying a cup of coffee in the mess before turning in. Another man was working on the second deck and was killed by flying debris. The bodies of the men lost in the gun turret had not been recovered. One injured man was still in critical condition. As the men watched somberly, each of them had the same thought: *that could have been me.*

Survival was just a matter of luck.

The deceased had been sewn into the shrouds, weighted down by five-inch gun shells. The ship's two chaplains conducted the service. Several prayers were recited, and the hymn "Eternal Father, Strong to Save" was sung:

Eternal Father, strong to save,
Whose arm hath bound the restless wave,
Who bid'st the mighty ocean deep,
Its own appointed limits keep;
Oh, hear us when we cry to Thee,
For those in peril on the sea.

The bodies rested on wooden slabs along the edge of the hangar deck. On the order, those boards were simultaneously tilted, consigning the bodies to the sea.

A seven-man Marine honor guard fired three volleys.

Watching from behind the Marine honor guard, Sprague and Reynolds held their salute. Then they went back to work.

Immediately following this ceremony, friends of the men were below, packing up their belongings in seabags to be sent home. Sailors were expert at cramming important parts of their lives into a very small space. Bunks and sea lockers had to be emptied. In addition to clothing, T-shirts, underwear, and socks, there were photographs, presumably of wives, children, and parents, some half-read books that would never be finished, letters, one diary that included a half-finished entry about the success at Truk, some knickknacks probably intended as gifts, and the most painful discovery, a medal of St. Christopher—the patron saint of travelers—on a chain. It was hard not to wonder, would anything have changed if he had been wearing it?

It was a sad and tedious process. One dilemma was what to do with opened packs of cigarettes? Pack 'em up and ship them home? Even if they got there, they'd be stale. Instead, one group of friends distributed the cigarettes and had a last smoke in the man's honor.

While emergency repairs were being made throughout the ship, Navy brass in Washington and Pearl Harbor were devising a strategy to get her home. Messages were bouncing back and forth, encoded to prevent the enemy from learning the full extent of the damage. *Intrepid* was wounded. She had lost the protection of the task force. Her engines were not damaged, so she could make 22 knots, more if absolutely necessary. But the ship had lost the ability to maneuver. It was stranded out in the Pacific.

Task Force 58 commander Admiral Ray Spruance, nicknamed "electric brain" for his coolness and decision-making under pressure, had created a smaller task group, designated 58.2.4, to escort *Intrepid* to recently captured Eniwetok, 670 miles away. This task force consisted of the heavy cruiser *San Francisco*, the light carrier *Cabot*, the cruiser *Wichita*, and the battleships *Stembel*, *Stephen Potter*, *The Sullivans*, and the *Owen*.

Task Force 58.2.4 made an enticing target for Japanese bombers—if they could find it. While capable of packing a punch, it was not strong enough to prevent a large, determined air attack from getting to *Intrepid*. Early in the evening of February 19, the first blip showed up on radar. It was more than 20 miles away but moving closer. Ray Stone held his breath as he watched it move across his screen. At that distance, it was really hard to determine . . . It veered off. Okay, it was a friendly. He released his breath.

Intrepid settled down for the night. Watches were set. Cards—and dice—and maybe a little ship-made alcohol came out. It was an attempt to get back to some semblance of normal. But it would never be normal for any of these sailors again. They had buried their shipmates a few hours earlier. It could have been them. They knew it. They rolled the dice.

On the bridge, Tom Sprague was exhausted. He'd been awake for almost 24 hours, and it didn't seem likely he was going to get any rest soon. Warship captains never sleep soundly. They lie down in their bunks, they close their eyes, but they never get too deeply asleep. So they create their own devices to fool themselves into staying sharp. Sprague was doing his best to keep up with his escorts, but it was almost impossible—he couldn't steer the damn thing.

SIX

THE KRIEGSMARINE'S FEARSOME battleship *Bismarck* was symbolic of the military and economic power of Hitler's Third Reich. *Bismarck* and her sister ship *Tirpitz* were the largest battleships ever built in Europe, the pride of the German navy, a massive 792 feet long and 118 feet across, armed with 8 highly accurate 15-inch guns and other armaments. *Bismarck*'s 3 turbines, 3 propellers, and 2 rudder assemblies enabled it to carry a crew of almost 2,000 men 9,000 nautical miles at 30 knots. At her christening ceremony in 1940, Hitler reminded Germans, "Six years after the National Socialist revolution, we are witnessing today the launching of . . . the largest battleship of our new fleet. I can give it no better name from our historical past . . . than the creator of that German Reich whose foresight has provided us now with the means for resurrection from bitter adversity and the wonderful expansion of the nation."

In May 1941, KMS *Bismarck* sailed into the North Atlantic, accompanied by the heavy cruiser *Prinz Eugen*. While entering the Denmark Strait, *Bismarck*'s electronically operated steering mechanism suddenly and inexplicably jammed; for

several seconds, the ship was out of control. Captain Ernst
Lindemann coolly prevented it from slamming into *Prinz
Eugen* by shouting commands to the helm, ordering them to
steer by adjusting power to the screws.

It was close call and quickly forgotten. A minor glitch on
what promised to be a glorious mission for the Fatherland.
"Our objective," Admiral Günther Lütjens, commanding the
convoy, told the crew, "is commerce-raiding in the Atlantic, imperiling England's existence." They would attack and
destroy Allied shipping bringing desperately needed supplies
from America to England. Without those American ship-
ments, Britain might not survive.

The Royal Navy set out to blunt the threat.

The two ships, *Bismarck* and *Prinz Eugen*, were initially spotted in Norwegian waters on May 21, preparing to break out into
the Atlantic. The British battlecruiser HMS *Hood*, the battleship
Prince of Wales, and several destroyers were ordered to intercept
them. "The Mighty" *Hood*, as she was known, was the pride of
the British war fleet. During *Bismarck*'s sea trials, its crew had
described the *Hood* as "the terror of the war games."

At 0545 on the morning of the 24th, the epic battle between the two great warships began in the Denmark Strait.
But less than four minutes after the opening salvos were fired,
one of *Bismarck*'s shells ripped into *Hood*'s ammunition magazine; 1,400 men died almost instantly in the massive explosions.
Only three sailors survived.

It was among the greatest naval disasters in the Royal
Navy's long, proud history.

It had taken KMS *Bismarck* only a few minutes to become
legend. Hitler was euphoric, awarding Germany's highest

honor, the Knight's Insignia of the Iron Cross, to the ship's head gunnery officer. News of the destruction of the *Hood* and its crew devastated Britain—and reinforced the growing fear throughout the world that Hitler's military was invincible. *Prince of Wales* was also hit in the fighting but managed to flee to safety. The British admiralty grasped the situation: *Bismarck* had to be stopped—whatever the cost.

The aircraft carriers *Victorious* and *Ark Royal*, three battleships, a battlecruiser, and four smaller cruisers were ordered to intercept and engage *Bismarck*. Just before midnight on the 24th, Swordfish torpedo planes from *Ark Royal* attacked under cover of a raging squall. The Fairey Swordfish was a fabric-covered biplane with an open cockpit, a gnat attacking an elephant. Its only advantage against the world's most sophisticated battleship was that it flew much too slowly for German radar to pick it up. One of the attackers dropped its torpedo from 500 yards away, only 20 feet above the water. By the time the plane was spotted, it was too late. As the heavily armored *Bismarck* made a desperate turn, the torpedo plowed into its exposed stern, destroying its steering gear— and jamming the rudders 12 degrees to port. *Bismarck* could only sail in wide, lazy circles. *Bismarck* was trapped; it couldn't maneuver, it couldn't get away from the rapidly approaching British armada.

Admiral Lütjens tried desperately to regain at least partial control. If only he could get back to Norway, he knew, the ship might be saved. They tried desperately to make emergency repairs. But structural damage and flooding prevented divers from getting into the steering room. The divers managed to straighten one of the two rudders, but the other one could not be freed. An officer suggested that they blow off the jammed rudder, to which the dejected admiral replied, "Do what you like; I am through with it."

Lütjens tried to steer the ship by alternating thrust to its propellers, but the design of the ship and stormy seas made that impossible. He briefly considered trying to sail backwards to the French coast, but just as quickly dismissed that thought. They were out of ideas. He sent a message to Hitler: "Ship unmaneuverable; we shall fight to the last shell."

The Royal Navy pressed the attack. *Bismarck* fought back, but escape was impossible. The jammed rudder had doomed the ship. She was pummeled by revenge-seeking British warships and carrier planes. It was blasted again and again and again. Aboard *Bismarck*, it was bedlam: some crewmen jumped into the sea. Officers supposedly committed suicide—or shot seamen who refused to stay at their posts. Men were trapped belowdecks by sealed hatches and doors. At 1037, the cruiser *Dorsetshire* fired three torpedoes, the final shots that tore into the hull. Great cheers went up aboard the British warships as *Bismarck* was sunk.

The Associated Press reported, "She had been pursued and harried for 1750 miles by a vast concentration of Royal Navy units afloat and in the skies until at last, crippled and whirling crazily and trapped and already mortally hit, she was sent to the bottom.

"Thus was the *Hood* avenged, in such a furious display of British naval might as has not been seen before in this war . . ." Of the more than 2,000 men aboard the German battleship, there were only 114 survivors.

Bismarck's fate was the nightmare of every warship captain from every navy in the world. They studied the battle.

They searched for some solution that had evaded Lütjens. On some level, they could relate to his helplessness. They could feel it. Many of them probably ran scenarios in their minds: *What would I do in that situation?* The answer was that there were no good answers.

That might not have been the first thought that ran through Tom Sprague's mind when *Intrepid* was hit, but it certainly must have popped up as soon as he saw the gyros tumble. The loss of the specific information the gyros provided—primarily course and stability—was not nearly as important as the meaning: *we're in desperate trouble.*

The failure of the gyros meant he had lost control of the ship. In those first few minutes, it was impossible to know the nature and extent of the damage, or even if it was just a temporary blip. Just that the ship was out of control.

Almost immediately, the helmsman confirmed it, telling Sprague what he already knew: she was not answering.

If he had taken a few seconds to think about it, he might have recalled that one of his favorite authors, John Dos Passos, had provided a pretty accurate description of the situation in the novel he had only recently finished reading, *Adventures of a Young Man*: "It was dark; they had a hard time finding their way through the woods . . . The mosquitoes ate the hides off them. 'Well, we're up shit creek without a paddle.'"

Intrepid had been turning left when she was hit, and that turn continued smoothly—without any direction from the helm. Sprague knew that meant the rudder had been jammed or locked into position. The left turn would never end.

Within minutes, the initial reports from damage control confirmed catastrophic damage to the steering assembly. It was only one torpedo, one unbelievably lucky—or unlucky, to the men of *Intrepid*—shot, hitting the ship in its most vulnerable place below the waterline. Had it struck almost anyplace else on the ship, the damage could have been absorbed and even repaired without affecting the ship's performance. Eight minutes after the explosion, damage control had isolated several compartments, including the aft steering room. Sprague was at the helm, trying to get a feel for what he could do to control the ship with the engines.

During training exercises, the Navy had piled problems on top of problems, testing a man's response as system after system failed. Trying to find his breaking point. Some people had complained, too much. Not Tom Sprague, though. He had enjoyed it, curious to see how well he could deal with a cascade of highly technical failures. Those years of preparation, that endless training, was paying off. He was more than able to handle multiple challenges. Even while trying to regain control of his ship, Sprague remained fully aware the enemy was still out there in the night, hunting. His only advantage was that the Japanese did not know, could not know—yet— that *Intrepid* was wounded and vulnerable.

The reality was that they were in *Bismarck* territory, unable to maneuver and protected by only a thin screen of destroyers. If the enemy found them . . .

He refused to let that possibility influence his decisions. If that happened, when that happened, he'd deal with it. While Reynolds's damage control teams were securing the ship, the rest of the crew stayed at their battle stations. In the CIC, Ray Stone and the other radar technicians kept their eyes locked on their screens. With luck, nothing would show up. But luck had proved to be pretty fickle.

Sprague continued experimenting with his engines. Eniwetok was 600 miles dead ahead, directly into the wind. They could make it—if the enemy didn't find them first. Applying full power to the two port engines and stop to one third on the starboard engines gave him some control—but it was tricky. He had to maintain at least 20 knots. At anything less than full power on the left engines, the ship would swing left.

The problem was the jammed rudder. The damage could not be repaired at sea. They were going to have to find workarounds.

A rudder is a small piece of equipment of massive importance. Basically, it's a flat or curved surface at the back of a boat that can be turned left or right to direct water flow, causing the bow to move in the opposite direction. It's almost always a metal or wooden fin controlled by the steering gear. The larger the ship, the larger the rudder it requires. The effectiveness of the rudder depends on the strength of the flow created by the ship's engines. The stronger the current, the more easily the ship will be moved.

After ancient mariners learned how to catch the winds in cloth sails, they invented the rudder to navigate. Rudders are believed to have evolved from handheld oars into paddles positioned on the side of the boat into an attached fin on the stern. The rudimentary technology dates back thousands of years to China's Han dynasty. The largest ships of Zheng He's treasure fleet had 36-foot-long wooden steering posts that connected to an enormous rudder, estimated to be as much as 450 square feet.

Few sailors pay attention to the rudder—until it fails. A ship without a rudder is like an arrow without feathers. It is directed by wind and currents. Or fate: it is not recorded in the Bible that Noah's Ark, had a rudder; instead, it apparently was guided through the flood by the hand of God.

Sprague and Reynolds had learned about rudders at the academy. Lessons that undoubtedly were punctuated by examples of rudders failing. The 74-gun HMS *Invincible*, for example, was built by the French in 1744 and captured by the British three years later, immediately becoming the largest warship in the British armada. She had a narrow, vertical rudder almost 36 feet long, enabling her to turn quickly and sharply—and her innovative design became the model for British warships for half a century. *Invincible* was considered one of the most technically advanced ships of the time. But in 1758, only miles outside Portsmouth, its anchor became wedged on the bottom. During efforts to free it, the rudder got jammed, and as its crew watched helplessly, their ship drifted onto a sandbar and could not be freed. Its 600 men and all 74 guns were saved, but after four days of flooding, the ship sank.

Damaged, jammed, and lost rudders remained a dire threat to ships, and there was no practical solution. Only in rare instances was the problem overcome: during a high-stakes tea clipper race in 1872 between the legendary *Cutty Sark* and *Thermopylae*, for example, *Cutty Sark*, which was well ahead, lost its rudder in a storm. The ship's carpenter literally forged a new rudder on deck, which somehow was attached to the stern, enabling her to safely reach London weeks after the victorious *Thermopylae*.

The increased use of torpedoes, fired by submarines or dropped by torpedo bombers, had made ships more vulnerable. Ironically, in February 1942, the German heavy cruiser

Prinz Eugen—which had been with *Bismarck* almost a year earlier when it destroyed the *Hood*, then was sunk by the Royal Navy—had its rudder blown off by the British submarine *Trident* off the coast of Norway. By using its propellers to maneuver, the ship managed to reach port, where two temporary rudders were installed. But rather than being operated mechanically from the bridge, these rudders had to be moved manually, literally requiring hands on deck to steer. Directions were shouted to them from the bridge. Relatively calm seas enabled *Prinz Eugen* to reach Kiel, Germany.

At Midway, two Japanese torpedoes ripped into *Yorktown* while it was taking evasive maneuvers, jamming its rudder at 15 degrees left and causing a total loss of power. Nothing could be done to save her, and 17 minutes after the torpedoes hit, the order was given to abandon ship.

Sprague had carefully read all the action reports in which ships had suffered rudder damage: *Bismarck*, *Prinz Eugen*, *Yorktown*, as well as several smaller vessels. He even had spoken with several of *Yorktown*'s officers; they all agreed there was nothing Captain Elliott Buckmaster could have done to save his ship.

Now it was Sprague's turn. Now he had to deal with it. He relied on Phil Reynolds and several other men for suggestions, but he made the decisions. When the immediate emergency was over, he gathered several men he trusted on the bridge to discuss options. Sprague summed up the situation: up shit creek. "So let me hear some good ideas." Before anyone responded, he corrected himself. They were beyond good ideas. He was open to anything at all.

Someone mentioned the ingenious solution that had saved the *Prinz Eugen*, in which crewmembers had manually moved the rudder by pulling a rope wound around a capstan. It was an amazing, impressive feat, steering an 18,000-ton warship by hand. Phil Reynolds shook his head. "No," he said. He had already discussed that possibility with members of his damage control team. "It won't work," he said. *Intrepid*'s rudder was jammed, maybe even bent into one of the screws. Even if they could attach a line to it, "which we cannot," he emphasized, "there's no way of freeing it. Forget it, we're not getting that rudder to move."

XO Rick Gaines told the story he'd heard of how an ingenious tugboat captain had saved a massive cruise ship. In the 1920s, the large passenger ship—he couldn't remember its name or even where he'd read about it—lost its rudder in rough seas while crossing the Pacific. "I wish I could remember the details. It was a big newspaper story for a couple of days." The lives of more than a thousand passengers were at risk on a ship that couldn't be controlled. Other vessels raced to help. He looked around. "None of you guys know about this?"

No one spoke up.

A day later, a tug reached the ship, Gaines continued. It was far too big to tow in the ocean, "So what they did was they hooked the tug right to the ship's stern and used it a de facto rudder. The tug shut down its engines and used its own rudder to steer the passenger ship." When the cruise ship wanted to go to starboard, the tug's rudder was set to port. Using this method, they maintained control at speeds as high as 18 knots all the way to Portsmouth.

Sprague actually considered it—for a few seconds. It wasn't a totally crazy idea. It would be incredibly complicated, even if *Intrepid* was capable of towing a destroyer. And he wasn't sure about that either. But, he decided, it was too dangerous without much chance of working. A tugboat was designed to make contact with other ships; no warship dared get that close to another, especially in rough seas. Nope.

Someone else, it might have been Tom Wallace, wondered aloud, "How about a paravane?" Paravanes, torpedo-shaped devices that can be towed underwater, had proved very useful during the First World War to protect against anchored mines. Paravanes were extended tautly from the bow on both sides of the ship by wires at a fixed depth; those wires were strong enough to cut a mine's mooring cable, releasing the mine to float to the surface, where sharpshooters waited to blow it up.

But paravanes also could be rigged to create drag. If only one paravane was put in the water, they might be able to rig it to compensate for the rudder angle.

The group discussed it seriously for several minutes. Sprague was intrigued. A paravane creates a very strong pull on its towing cable—strong enough to cut a mooring cable—and if it were let out on the leeward side, the side opposite the wind, it would keep *Intrepid*'s bow out of the wind, making it easier to use the engines to steer. It was an interesting theory, but getting it right would require considerable experimentation to figure out how big it would have to be, and they had neither the time nor the materials.

There was, of course, one other technique that had been used almost from the beginning of recorded history to steer ships: sail. Ancient mariners had learned how to adjust their rigging, the array of sails, to catch the wind, and in conjunction with oars or paddles along the side, direct their ship. The academy graduates had studied the history at Annapolis, and several of them had even been members of the sailing club, but all of the men in this group were experienced sailors. They knew the feeling of ripping through the day in a stiff breeze, spray blowing in your face, using the tiller to move the rudder and steer the boat. Being in control of your fate.

But that knowledge wasn't much use in this situation. You can't sail a 40,000-ton aircraft carrier.

The small force headed for Eniwetok, almost dead ahead. Running the two port engines at full power while reducing or shutting down the starboard engines enabled them to maintain a relatively direct course. From time to time, every man on the bridge would steal a glance at the gauges, making certain those engines were running smoothly. So far, so . . .

Back in Pearl, the brass was trying to figure out how to get *Intrepid* home, where it could be repaired and put back in action as quickly as possible. Only a few Allied leaders knew why that was so important. In Washington, preparations were underway for the most challenging and secret operation of the war, Operation Overlord, the invasion of Europe.

It had always been difficult to maintain a balance between the fight against the Nazis in Europe and the Japanese in Asia. There had been a continuing competition for men, supplies, and equipment. And since the allies had regained the offensive, the situation had become even more difficult. The outcome of the war against Hitler was going to be decided on the beaches of Europe, almost definitely somewhere on the French coast, the shortest route across the English Channel. If the allies gained a foothold, they could fight their way to Berlin. But that was a huge if. Accomplishing that required building the greatest invasion force in history, and so men and equipment were being diverted from the war in the Pacific. *Intrepid*, with its 100 planes, was going to be needed. The damage it had suffered was not catastrophic; the rudder could be quickly replaced. Getting safely to dry dock in Hawaii or even San Francisco was the challenge.

Intrepid limped towards Eniwetok. Sprague didn't understand why they were being sent there. The atoll had just been captured; in fact, in certain areas, enemy troops were still holding out. There were no facilities there capable of making even rudimentary repairs to the ship. But Tom Sprague had been dutifully following orders for more than a quarter century; he wasn't about to start questioning them now.

Sprague guessed the brass just wanted him to get into a safe harbor until they could figure out how to proceed.

Throughout the day on February 18, the skies remained bright, blue, and clear of enemy airplanes. The storms of the past few days had passed. The guess was that the Japanese were searching for the fleet, trying to figure out Admiral Montgomery's next objective, and might not even be aware this small force had broken off. The few blips that showed up on radar screens created moments of anxiety, but all of them proved to be friendlies.

It was difficult not to think about *Bismarck*. A jammed rudder had doomed that ship. *Intrepid* was still able to defend itself; planes could be launched from the catapults, and the ship's guns were loaded and manned. But a ship that cannot maneuver is exceedingly vulnerable.

Sprague stayed in contact with the brass as much as possible, but extensive radio communications risked alerting the

Japanese to their situation and position. Admiral Spruance had provided as much protection as the task force could spare, but it wasn't nearly enough to fight off a sustained enemy attack. There was nothing more Washington could do to help. The not knowing, the wondering, the speculation was taxing. About all they could do was watch the sky and hope their luck held out.

The funerals had been difficult; every man had stopped whatever they were doing, wherever they were, when "Taps" was broadcast through the speakers. It was a somber few moments, and some men cried, but then the ship came back to life. The crew continued cleaning up debris and making repairs. A net was strung up on the hangar deck, and the volleyball games resumed. The movie, a comedy entitled *This Is the Army* starring Ronald Reagan, was shown in a rec room but was poorly attended. Several men got the date February 17 tattooed on their arms, their way of marking their first day under enemy fire. It was a Friday, so the mess served more than 3,000 portions of fish. But many men had been at or near their stations for more than 24 hours, so they grabbed sack time.

Several men had picked up small pieces of the torpedo and were keeping them as souvenirs. Commander Gaines requested they turn them in, writing, "Analysis of a sufficient number of pieces will serve to identify the type of torpedo . . . enabling experts to determine whether this is a known type or a new type which the enemy has not used before. This information is essential to those designing the protective features of ships . . .

"Please turn these souvenirs in to the Gunnery officer."

The ship stayed steady on an 065 heading toward Eniwetok, maintaining a speed between 20 and 22 knots. As long as they stayed at that speed, they were able to keep the yaw, basically the side-to-side swinging, at no more than 15 degrees to port or starboard. It wasn't ideal, but it was doable. It would get them to safe harbor.

If the situation was not normal aboard, at least there was an imitation of normalcy. Life moved on. Those few moments of terror, when the ship was out of control and heading straight for *Essex*, were stored forever in memories. It would make a great story—someday.

In an attempt to boost morale, the daily orders included, "An Open Message to Tojo: You think your boys threw a little scare into us last night, don't you? Well, you see, Tojo, as always you don't understand Americans. You thought a new ship and crew would be 'duck soup' for you, but you just couldn't know it was INTREPID men you were tangling with. This time, Tojo, you went too far, 3000 of us are out for revenge and your blood.

"We have already left a dent in your hide you will never forget. But next time, Oh Boy! You see, Tojo—we're tough—we're INTREPID and we'll be back."

On the morning of February 19, Sprague was having a third cup of coffee in his cabin when a coded message was received from Pearl Harbor. A course change: rather than Eniwetok, *Intrepid* was to proceed directly to Majuro, the largest city in the Marshall Islands. That made sense. Majuro had been occupied by the Army and Marines without resistance on January 31, the first day of the campaign. One of the 64 small islands in the atoll, it had a 400-foot timber

pier, a seaplane ramp, and a 5,800-foot runway—and a protected lagoon 200 feet deep in places.

"This is the Captain speaking," Sprague announced, a
little more bounce than usual in his voice. "We've just been
given a new destination. We are going to Majuro. They've
got a deep, safe harbor there where we will receive assistance
not available at Eniwetok. I'll let you know about any further changes." Then he added, "Keep it up, men, you're
doing a fine job."

The new course was quickly plotted, but actually making the correction without a rudder was considerably more
complicated. Sprague and Reynolds continually adjusted
engine thrust to turn the ship. It required a combination
of experience and experiment, trial and error, reducing
power to the port engines and letting the locked rudder
move the ship to starboard, then powering up again to
maintain that position.

In different circumstances, this would have been the type
of interesting problem that Sprague enjoyed solving. Making the course correction was difficult and time-consuming.
Keeping it on the new course was close to impossible.

The problem was the wind. As a pilot and a sailor, Tom
Sprague understood and appreciated the majesty and the mysteries of the wind. Like all those who fly or go to sea, his life
often depended on that knowledge. Wind was nature's most
powerful tool; it could assist or destroy on a whim. Wind
literally lifted planes into the air, but entire fleets had simply
disappeared in the wind.

Back in flight school in Pensacola, when fliers were just
figuring how to deal with the winds, they liked to quote the

Chinese proverb, "When the winds of change blow, some people build walls and others build windmills." In other words, you can fight it or use it. There were other sayings too from those days, but they weren't as polite. An instructor, Scotty MacGregor, used to twirl the tips of his mustache, shake his head, and muse to young fliers, "She's a tricky bitch, that one, don't ever trust her. Just as soon kiss ya as kill ya."

Sprague had seen what the winds could do. On a sunny, still September afternoon years ago, he was watching a friend make an ordinary landing when a wind shear spun out of nowhere—out of nowhere, without warning—to catch his biplane and corkscrewed him into the ground.

Veteran pilots had taught him to respect the wind; rather than fighting it, figure out how to use it. In his own career, he'd been blown around enough—both on land and sea—to know how true that was.

The new course put the wind on their port side. It was blowing a steady 30 knots, almost 35 miles per hour. An optimist would call that a strong breeze. A pessimist would refer to it as a near gale. Sailors might describe it as "a good blow."

They played with the engines, trying to get in harmony with the wind and the sea, trying different combinations like a chef adding spices, a little more of this, a little less of that. The ship had not been designed for that level of stress. Running the engines at full speed, then backing off, coupled with the damage to the hull created serious vibration, like tapping a tuning fork. Pipes throughout the ship picked up that tune and resisted it.

After several hours, pipes in the engine room were compromised. They began leaking at the joints. Sprague had to make an impossible choice. He had to take some of the strain off the engines, but if he reduced speed, he would lose what little control they still had.

An aircraft carrier, with its long flat deck and massive control island on one side, is asymmetrical, woefully unbalanced. The island, the massive structure rising high above the flight deck on the starboard side, in which all the essential control systems are situated, acts essentially as a mainsail, causing the ship to be pushed and shoved by the prevailing winds. Rather than weight being roughly evenly distributed down the centerline, like a battleship or cruiser, carriers rely on ballast tanks filled with water on the side opposite the island to maintain an even trim.

The strong winds complicated an already complex equation. *Intrepid* refused to be harnessed. "She was sashaying like the hips of one of those hula girls back in Pearl," as Gordon Keith described it. On the bridge, the helmsman stood in position, his arms at his sides, resisting the temptation to put his hands on the now useless wheel.

Meanwhile, the officers continued adjusting the engines to compensate as much as possible for the swinging bow. Sprague had ordered the outer starboard shaft locked, which reduced the arc but did not prevent the ship from swinging to the left. The escort destroyers *Stembel* and *Stephen Potter* stayed well clear of the ship.

In a somewhat desperate attempt to restore some control, it was decided to attach steel cables from those destroyers to *Intrepid*; the hope was those cables could be stretched to keep the carrier in position between the two escorts. In theory, it made sense, but with the seas bubbling high and rough, no one had the slightest idea how it would translate into reality.

Late in the afternoon, the destroyers eased close enough to *Intrepid* to try to attach the cables. It was a difficult and dangerous maneuver. *Stembel*'s captain described it as trying to saddle a bucking bronco in a hurricane. They had to back off several times before they were able to pass the chains across. For a time, the cables provided a minimum of control, stretching and slacking back and forth as the bow swung, managing to keep the carrier on a wide zigzag course towards Majuro.

As Sprague later explained the situation to Navy brass, "She was like a giant pendulum, swinging back and forth . . . She had a tendency to weathercock into the wind . . . turning her bow towards Tokyo."

"But right then I wasn't interested in going in that direction."

Ironically, the techniques of sailing were not part of the curriculum when Sprague and Reynolds attended Annapolis. By the turn of the 20th century, the Navy had completed its transition from sail to steam. The last of the large sailing ships used to train midshipmen had sunk at its dock in 1912 and had not been replaced. Rather than the traditional summer sailing cruise, young sailors learned rudimentary seamanship techniques in small boats: sloops called half-raters, catboats, and 26-foot cutters equipped with spars and sails.

The knowledge of centuries, the science and art of catching and utilizing the winds, slowly was being allowed to disappear. But Sprague had been intrigued by it. Growing up, he must have been enchanted by seafaring literature, from Richard Henry Dana's memoir *Two Years Before the Mast* to Melville's *Moby Dick*. In late-night debates at the academy about the virtues of powered boats over sailing ships, he had cautioned his classmates not to ignore the past in their new-found excitement about the future.

As they were all aware, the same fundamentals of physics applied to sailing any type of ship. Weight, weather, wind, waves, displacement, depth, and a hundred other factors were just the beginning of figuring it out. The one thing Sprague knew for certain about *Intrepid*'s situation was that he couldn't power his way out of it. Even the ship's massive engines could no longer compensate for the loss of steering. How was he going to control the ship? Essentially, he slowly began to realize, *Intrepid* had to be controlled using the same techniques as the sailing ships that once had captured his imagination.

Although admittedly there was no way of knowing how that science might apply to a 40,000-ton ship. Or if it was even possible.

While some specifics are lost to history—in the haste to save the ship nobody paused to make a record—it's possible to piece the events and make a strong supposition of how this actually happened. Sprague apparently brought up his idea to Phil Reynolds, although at first he didn't use the word *sail*. "We need to find some way to stop the wind from pushing us around," he said in the vaguest possible terms. He knew how crazy this concept sounded.

"What do you have in mind?" Reynolds responded.

Sprague told him. "Okay," he began, "we know what the problem is. The island acts like the mainsail of a schooner. The wind pushes on it. Suppose we could find a way of compensating for that. You know, maybe rigging some kind of . . ." he hesitated, then said it, ". . . sail."

Reynolds smiled. A sail? Rig a sail that would deflect the wind? That would have to be some big sail, and they didn't even carry small sails.

Even if they could find a sail and rig it, another huge if, it was impossible to know if it would make the slightest difference. Historically, the mainsail generally was the largest part of the rigging. It was hung from the main mast to catch the wind and propel the boat. In photographs of the great sailing ships, it was usually seen fully puffed out, billowing gracefully in the wind.

At first Reynolds didn't believe Sprague was serious; he figured he was just throwing out a wild, improbable idea to spark some creative thinking. He did that sometimes to generate discussion. The best ideas, he'd once said, came at the end of a back-and-forth discussion. Reynolds didn't scoff openly at the suggestion. You don't scoff at the captain. Instead he agreed with the most obvious points. The carrier's island certainly was the highest point in a carrier and did deflect the wind. No one could debate that.

But he was surprised when Sprague continued talking about it, as if it actually could be done.

The two men sat comfortably in Sprague's cabin for the next 15, 20 minutes. Reynolds admired Sprague. He considered him a smart, innovative, complex thinker, a practical adventurer with a mechanic's education and a daredevil's courage.

But this? Come on. You can't sail an aircraft carrier. No one could debate that either.

Reynolds asked the obvious, logical questions, poking the holes necessary to deflate the idea. Instead, the captain had answers for some of them. For others he said simply, "We'll figure it out." The more Sprague spoke about this idea, the more his enthusiasm for it grew, and the more he envisioned it. Gradually, the crazy idea became more realistic—like a sail filling slowly with the breeze.

Sprague requested several other officers meet them on the bridge. Like Reynolds, initially they thought he was kidding. But then his idea began to billow. "Look at this," he explained, drawing a rough sketch on the back of a chart to illustrate what he had in mind, "we've got to blunt the rudder effect, we can do that by deflecting the wind with some kind of headsail."

They huddled around the chart table and looked at his sketch. The conversation progressed from absurd to interesting to the possible. On paper, it actually made sense. Rick Gaines shrugged and said, "You know what, I've actually seen some crazier ideas."

"How many of them worked?" asked one of the other men.

Gaines nodded. "Well, some of them."

Gradually, the group overcame their initial skepticism. Rigging sails on an aircraft carrier was crazy and they all knew it, but Captain Sprague was trying to apply the physics of sailing to the present condition of the ship. That made a lot of sense. Essentially, what he wanted to do was lower the ship's profile, which would alleviate some of the pressure on the mainsail, on the island.

Disdain gradually morphed into consideration and grew slowly into enthusiasm. No matter how unusual it was, anything that changed the current equation was welcome. The small group wasn't fully committed to it, but they began discussing how it actually might get done. The question was how to "rig a jib," as one of the officers put it. A headsail, or foresail as it is sometimes referred to, is a sail on the bow that can be used to deflect the wind. A jib is a smaller headsail.

Rick Gaines had sat mostly quiet during the meeting. Jigsaw puzzles had become popular in America in the 1930s because they were an inexpensive and challenging form of entertainment. He had brought a couple of them aboard with him, guessing he might have hours to fill. One of them depicted the presidential carvings on the recently completed Mount Rushmore. The other one was a rainy night on the Champs-Élysées. It had been a more eventful journey than expected; he hadn't even had time to open the boxes. But Sprague was proposing a different kind of puzzle: How do you make the ship smaller? How do you reduce the surface exposed to the port winds?

"How about this?" Gaines finally said. In unison, everyone turned to face him. He was playing with some figures on a clipboard. "Right now, we've got about 65 planes on the flight deck. We can get another 20 up there pretty quick. Suppose we just move all of them forward, right to the front of the bow?" He tapped his pencil on the pad and looked at Sprague, "Hellcats weigh almost 9,000 pounds apiece. The Avengers are what, twice that? All that weight would definitely push down the bow."

Sprague looked around the room, waiting for a response. No one voiced any objections. Tom Wallace threw up his hands. "It's a start." Lowering the bow would reduce the surface exposed to the wind.

There was nothing to lose. "All right, Rick," Sprague said. "How do we move all those planes?"

Gaines smiled, the first time he had smiled in several days, and replied, "Very carefully."

It took a mammoth effort to get it done. Moving airplanes on the flight deck of an aircraft carrier deck can be tricky even in calm seas. Moving dozens of them simultaneously on a swaying deck in stormy seas against a persistently strong wind is an almost Herculean task, requiring brute strength and delicate balance. Imagine trying to fit a Sherman tank into a tight parking space between two Fords in a shopping center lot. The fuel tanks of these planes were drained just in case, but it was still dangerous. The last thing the ship could afford at this point was a plane rolling free on a densely crowded flight deck.

Seven or eight men were assigned to each plane. Hundreds of off-duty sailors converged on the flight deck to assist the airdales, the experienced plane handlers who directed the choreography. One by one, the Hellcats and Avengers, their wings folded, were rolled into position and chained down on the bow.

There were a few incidents. Two sailors got into it and had to be separated when the planes they were moving brushed wingtips. Several toes were broken or bruised when wheels ran over them. But overall, the repositioning went surprisingly well. Within several hours, a fleet of airplanes was parked in long rows on the bow.

While this was taking place, Sprague also ordered the stern trimmed. The back of the ship already was riding low in the Pacific because of the hull damage caused by the torpedo, and the several flooded compartments drove it down even lower. He also ordered as much cargo as possible moved aft to add weight. His hope was that lowering the stern would give the screws, the propellers, more bite, giving them more control.

Then they held their breath. If they got a break, if the

winds eased just a bit and did not change direction, they would be able to make it to Majuro.

Shifting all that weight aft cut down the swaying, and shutting down the outer #1 shaft eliminated at least some of the troublesome vibration. The leaks were sealed. The situation wasn't ideal, but it had reached tolerable. With help from the escorting destroyers, *Intrepid* reached the island and was guided into the calm waters of the lagoon.

It was a brief stop, just long enough to take a deep breath and confirm that nothing could be done, even temporarily, to repair the rudder. Within hours, the ship was resupplied and took on fresh water. They also sent an honor guard ashore to bury the final man killed in the attack in the atoll's Pejerian Cemetery.

From there *Intrepid* was ordered to head "straight" to Pearl Harbor, about 2,400 miles away, although, as Sprague mused, "straight was quite an optimistic description." They had done just about everything they could think of to gain some control of the ship; Sprague guessed the officers gathered on the bridge had a cumulative total of a little more than 200 years of naval experience. There wasn't much at least one of them hadn't seen, done, or been through. Until now. This was a first for all of them. Together they had done a good job, though, and the crew had been spectacular. They had dutifully performed every task, even if they weren't quite sure exactly why it was being done. They trusted their captain. That was enough.

Intrepid could not go "'straight" to Pearl Harbor. Maintaining a desired heading was impossible, but as Sprague said later, it did have one advantage: "No enemy sub could have ever figured out her zig-zag plan. The course or pattern was created as we went along, and no one knew for sure how long she'd keep on anything like a straight course."

As they departed Majuro, it appeared the steps they had taken had been effective, although the destroyer escorts remained wary in case *Intrepid* suddenly swerved left or right. After one such unexpected move that almost caused a collision, *Stembel* signaled, "Please let us know when you make your next unannounced course change."

The crew adapted to the sudden abrupt movements, fully aware of the dangers. Captain Sprague's aide, Tony Zollo, wrote his own description in his diary: "If this was a car on a highway, the driver would be arrested for drunk driving and weaving from one side of the road to the other."

Several other crew members suggested that the best way to deal with it was to actually start drinking, which might compensate for the swaying, making it feel normal.

But it worked. It wasn't ideal, and they were in for a bumpy ride, but it worked. They were able to maintain sufficient control over the ship that Sprague felt comfortable enough to lie down in his bunk for an hour or maybe two.

And then, without warning, the winds shifted.

Only hours out of Majuro, the wind direction changed. The Pacific started playing with the carrier, pushing it, pulling it. Bobbing it like a child's boat in a bathtub. The escorts had to drop their cables and move farther away.

Sprague rushed back to the bridge. He was running out of ideas. As he got there, *Intrepid* suddenly shifted hard to port, almost sending him into the bulkhead. He grabbed a rail to maintain his balance. Phil Reynolds was already there. The two men stood shoulder to shoulder, watching with growing horror as the bow swayed violently.

"Any ideas?" Reynolds asked.

Finally, Sprague said aloud what both men were thinking: "I think we'd better find a fucking paddle."

SEVEN

A PADDLE.

Somehow, somewhere, they had to create a "paddle," a means to harness *Intrepid*.

There was a lesson in history. Long before the invention of the moveable rudder, men would propel and steer their rafts with their hands or by long poles pushed into shallow river bottoms. But soon the first sails, probably animal skins attached to a pole, allowed mariners to use the wind to carry them across deeper bodies of water.

Great sails, sails of reed matting or woven from cloth, allowed civilizations to explore and develop. Sprague wasn't suggesting a traditional sail that would propel the ship—*Intrepid*'s engines were not damaged—but rather a sail that could divert the winds that were making the ship uncontrollable. A sail to compensate for the jammed rudder.

Although Sprague had been the first person to mention it, even he hadn't considered it realistic. It was a broad concept. Just throwing out an idea. But an actual sail? No one was certain how that somewhat whimsical idea had morphed into an actual plan.

The fact that the ship did not carry any sails did not dissuade them.

The thought that it might be possible to employ an ancient technique to replace modern naval technology actually was not as bizarre as it sounded. A sail or sails had been used by modern ships in emergencies several times. By 1921, for example, America's new R-class submarines were the largest, most lethal, and most technologically advanced boats in the Navy's fleet. In May that year, the 2-year-old *R-14* was running smoothly on the surface, taking part in a massive search for the oceangoing tug *Conestoga*, which had disappeared. Almost 150 miles outside Hilo, Hawaii *R-14* suddenly lost power; to the crew's horror, they discovered all its useable fuel had been contaminated by seawater.

R-14 was dead in the ocean. Its batteries had been drained, meaning they also had lost use of their radio. They had no way of reporting their situation, no way to request help. The boat was floating alone, without power, lost somewhere in the Pacific.

Every sailor's nightmare.

With few options and limited supplies onboard, engineering officer Roy Gallemore proposed an outlandish plan to save the boat: rig a sail and let the wind carry them to safety.

There was nothing to lose by trying it. The crew built a frame from metal bunk bed railings and tied eight hammocks to it. They lashed the makeshift sail to the front of the conning tower. Then they waited for the wind.

Slowly, grudgingly, the 570-ton submarine began to move. It managed to reach 1.2 knots, enough to create "steerageway," a water flow strong enough to allow the rudder to steer the ship. It was working. The crew hung another sail, a mainsail made of six blankets, to the radio mast, increasing the sub's speed by an additional half knot. A third sail of eight blankets got their speed up to slightly more than 2 knots.

The wind propulsion turned the propellers, which allowed the generator to charge the batteries. *R-14* literally sailed for 64 hours until it safely reached Hilo Harbor.

The story of *R-14*'s amazing sail created a small and memorable sensation. This kind of innovative thinking—and doing—was studied throughout the Navy. Sails had mostly disappeared from American warships four decades earlier, a relic of the past, and by the beginning of the Roaring '20s, masts originally designed to hold sails were being used to mount various types of radar, fire control, and other equipment. The voyage of the *R-14* served as a nostalgic reminder of the glorious past to modern sailors.

Academy graduates Tom Sprague and Phil Reynolds undoubtedly knew the story. In fact, as their careers progressed, they most likely were aware of several other instances in which makeshift sails were used in emergencies as well. In 1925, for example, Commander John Rodgers, the Navy's second trained aviator, who literally had been taught to fly by the Wright brothers, had run out of fuel flying an experimental seaplane from San Francisco to Hawaii and had made an emergency landing in the ocean 200 miles from Maui. Rodgers and his four-man crew were stranded at sea.

A day later, as it became apparent the Navy did not know where they were, they created a makeshift sail by stripping the fabric covering from the plane's wings and tying it to the struts with antenna wire. They started sailing in the direction of Hawaii. Nine days later, a submarine spotted them off Kauai and rescued them.

Much more recently, in 1940, the destroyer USS *Tucker* was on picket duty near Wake Island, basically floating in place for several days. It was a tedious assignment, requiring them to burn a great amount of fuel keeping the ship's systems operating while actually going nowhere. As an experiment, an activity to keep the crew alert and involved in an otherwise prosaic exercise, Captain Hilyer Gearing decided to save some of that fuel by rigging sails to propel his ship.

His men sewed two large sails, a mainsail and a foresail, and fastened them to the two masts. The sails allowed the ship to make 3.4 knots as they circled on station—while successfully preserving a significant amount of fuel.

It was the kind of odd, peacetime antic that attracted a lot of attention, but it also served as a small reminder to sailors not to overlook their heritage.

Aboard *Intrepid*, the idea had finally taken hold. But Tom Sprague wasn't totally convinced. It would require a massive effort, and he wasn't sure it was worth it.

"It's an engineering problem," Rick Gaines explained. The small group had gathered in the captain's cabin. It was almost 0300, and visibility was less than 1,500 yards. "The wind is pushing us to port," he continued, roughing out another sketch; this one showed wind arrows impacting the ship outline on the right side, pushing it left. "If we can catch enough of that breeze to push us in the opposite direction, we can hold the bow reasonably straight."

"All right," Sprague said. "Assuming we do this, just assuming, where do you propose we hang this thing?"

Gaines, Reynolds, and Frank Johnson had already discussed this. There were several options. Johnson spoke up, "Captain, what makes the most sense is rigging it on the forward radio masts." Those masts were in front of the island, near the bow on the starboard side. Hanging a sail in there would greatly diminish the force of the wind actually hitting the island. "But that isn't going to work," he continued. "I went up there and looked at it. I looked at everything, trying to figure out how we could make this work. There's no way. Those masts aren't strong enough to support a sail filled with wind." He shook his head to emphasize the point. "They weren't designed to take that kind of stress."

"And even if they could," Reynolds added, "I don't know how the hell we'd rig them up there." The days of spritely young men clambering up the masts to attach sails were long gone. "There's got to be something better."

The design of the ship made it more complicated. While British and Japanese carriers had an enclosed hangar deck, the hangar deck on *Essex*-class carriers was open. There was logic behind it: it allowed planes to be warmed up below, a 15- to 20-minute process, then lifted up to the flight deck by elevator to quickly take off. The open hangar deck allowed potentially noxious fumes to dissipate—but it also meant the deck could be cold and very windy. It wasn't exactly a wind tunnel, not even close, and light steel roller doors could be closed to block much of the wind, but it wasn't airtight and still served as a path for the wind to buffet the ship.

The more serious problem was the open forecastle. The forecastle, also known as the fo'c'sle, is the most forward part of the ship. Historically, it was an enclosed "castle" at the front of the main deck on warships from which archers could fire arrows at enemy ships. But on carriers, the term had come to refer to the front of the hangar deck, the area where the anchor chains and the capstans, the machinery that winds the chains when the ship drops or lifts anchor, are located. For convenience, it too was open, meaning the anchor teams were exposed to the weather—and in rough seas, waves would break over the bow and often flood this area.

Without a rudder to maintain a course, the strong gusts swirling inside the fo'c'sle overwhelmed even the minimal control adjusting the engines provided.

"Okay, so hypothetically," Sprague asked, looking at Reynolds's sketch. "Hypothetically, tell me what good putting a sail there is going to do." He knew the answer but wanted to hear Reynolds's explanation.

"Hypothetically," Reynolds explained, a sail would block the wind action. Think of it as a length of pipe, he suggested. A gust blowing directly in front of it will flow right through it without moving it. But if the gust comes from the side, it strikes one side of the pipe, and if it is strong enough, it can turn the pipe. "It can spin it if it's strong enough."

"Like us," Johnson added.

"Like us," Reynolds agreed, then continued. "But if you close off the end of the pipe the wind's gonna have a pretty minimal effect. Make sense?"

Sprague stared at the paper, wondering if there were any alternatives they hadn't considered. In the last few hours, he had received several urgent messages from Pearl requesting status updates; it was obvious they did not appreciate the seriousness of the situation. They were asking when *Intrepid* would reach Hawaii, not the real question: How were they going to get there? They also made it clear there was no assistance they could offer.

Sprague did not answer the questions. "Assuming we do this," Sprague asked, tapping the sketch, "you have any idea how big this thing is going to have to be to make a difference?"

"Yeah," Reynolds acknowledged. "Big. Big as we can make it."

Tom Sprague had spent his entire naval career getting things done. The first step, he knew, was taking the first step. Debate was the antithesis of action. He'd seen potentially beneficial missions fail before they even got started because someone doubted it could be done. In the span of his own career, the Navy had gone from believing firmly a plane couldn't fly off a ship at sea to launching Jimmy Doolittle's miraculous carrier-based B-25B attack on Tokyo. In fact, it was Doolittle himself who had pointed out, "The only way to do it is to do it."

There wasn't an inch of the ship that these men did not know well. There were several other possible places a sail might be rigged. Suggestions were made and debated, pros and cons of each site discussed. There was no right answer. It was a lot of guesswork tempered by practicality and experience.

Sprague made the decision, relying on a warning he'd received decades earlier at the beginning of flight training: don't worry about your landing until you're off the ground. Good advice: focus on the present. Get going. "Okay," he said finally and firmly, "let's get this done."

There was no discussion. Whatever doubts any of them had, they said nothing. The captain wanted them to make and rig a sail. They would make and rig a sail. Somehow.

Sprague continued. "I think Frank's idea is right. Let's close off the fo'c'sle." The sail could be rigged to the overhead. There were numerous places to tie it down. They would figure that out. But if it worked, always that big if, it would prevent the wind from pushing the ship to port.

While this discussion was going on, Sprague's aide, Tony Zollo, arrived with another fresh pot of coffee. He poured half cups. Carefully. With the ship rocking, no one wanted to risk a brimming cup of hot coffee. Sprague couldn't guess how much coffee he had consumed in the previous 36 hours. Fifteen cups? More, definitely more. He was used to it; it was a fact of life in the Navy that the amount of sleep a man got was inversely proportional to rank and responsibility. He remained wary that lack of sleep might lead him to make poor decisions. Like making a sail, for example.

Oddly, though, the more he thought about it, the more sense it made to try this idea. They had to do something.

But, he decided, whatever happened, this one was on him. He was not going to inform the brass. Or request permission. He could always claim he couldn't risk letting the Japanese know how precarious his situation was. If it worked, people might talk about it, they might even study it at the academy— but they definitely were going to talk about it if it didn't work. And they would shake their heads and wonder whatever happened to Tom Sprague. How could he get talked into such a crazy idea?

No matter how it turned out, this was his responsibility; if it failed, he was going to take the blame. Phil Reynolds

picked up his coffee cup and offered a wishful toast. "Gentlemen, here goes nothing." And, naturally, warm coffee rolled
over the brim and stained his uniform.

Step one, done. The decision was made: They would rig
a sail. Now all they had to do was everything. They moved
to step two, putting the plan into action.

Half a century earlier, every ship carried a sailmaker
and often several assistants. The sailmaker was a skilled
craftsman, a vitally important and respected member of
the crew. The survival of the ship often depended on their
skills; warships required literally acres of sails, which could
be relied on in every type of weather to overtake the enemy
or escape pursuers when necessary. While the rating still
existed in the Navy, sailmakers no longer played an important role in the operation of a ship. Other than sewing
body bags, repairing hatch covers, and making hammocks,
there wasn't a lot of need for one.

Sprague actually knew a little bit about sailmaking. He'd
done his share of recreational sailing, especially early in his
career, but it wasn't a passion. Too much time spent waiting
to go too slow. He was more a "crank up the engine and let
'er rip" kind of guy. But he'd spent several years living down
in Pensacola, which had once been a favorite port for com-
mercial fishermen and ships carrying lumber to and from
Europe. As a result, the streets at the port were lined with
shops that provided the necessary support, from caulking to
provisions to repairing nets. Among the best known was the
Joseph Porter Sail Works.

Porter's sold and repaired sails. Just about every ship that
crossed the Atlantic needed rips, tears, and holes in their sails
repaired. There was a large workshop in the back where the

sewing was done, a lot of it by hand, and sailors were welcome to visit and share stories. Sprague loved sitting in that
room, listening to those sea stories and watching the experts
deftly making repairs. On occasion, they let him do some
basic stitching. So he knew it could be done.

Intrepid's sailmaker, 26-year-old Gordon Keith, was a
handsome, physically large man. "Flash" Gordon, as he
was known in deference to the comic book hero, had been
a three-year starter at tackle for Calhoun County High
School's football team. His classmates knew him as quiet
but determined; he showed up on time, did the job without
fuss, didn't need compliments, and got it done. Their class
motto, "Success is sweet, but the secret of success is work,"
accurately described the heartland values he had been taught
growing up in West Virginia.

Large parts of West Virginia were still suffering from the
aftermath of the Great Depression when Keith graduated in
1939. Calhoun was farm country, fruit and tobacco farms
mostly. There was a large textile factory one county over, but
Calhoun didn't have the rich coal lodes found in other areas
of the state, so good jobs were scarce. Weeks after his graduation, like several of his classmates, he enlisted in the Navy.

It was never quite clear to him how he became a sailmaker.
But that was the military: take a small-town boy from ru-
ral West Virginia and tell him he's suddenly a sailmaker. He
didn't know much about sailing other than the pictures he
had seen in *Life* and *The Saturday Evening Post*, and all he knew
about sewing was that his mother was really good at it. And
he had repaired her sewing machine several times. But when
the Navy said you were a sailmaker, you were a sailmaker.

He had learned the basics of the job and actually liked it. He was assigned two large compartments on the third deck, a canvas and fabric workshop and a storeroom behind the crew's mess near the stern, two mates to assist him, and two top-of-the-line Singer Zig Zag sewing machines. Best of all, though, stuck down there, near the back of the lower deck, officers rarely came around to hassle them.

They were always busy. In addition to those body bags, they made hatch covers, slings and hammocks, and a lot of sun canopies. While it wasn't part of the job description, if a guy needed a garment repaired, they would do that too, most often accepting a few loose cigarettes in payment.

So when the request came, he had absolutely no idea why Captain Sprague wanted to see him. *On the double! Don't take time to put on fresh dungarees.* As he climbed up to the bridge, he tried to figure out what he possibly could have done that required meeting with the captain. He had never met Sprague personally, but knew he was a good officer; he paid attention to his men.

Keith had never been on *Intrepid*'s bridge before. He'd never been up that high on any ship, so he tried not to look around as he reported.

Sprague returned his salute, then told him, "We've got a problem, and we need your help."

Everyone knew what the problem was: they couldn't steer the damn ship. *Intrepid* was rocking and rolling all over the place. But that couldn't be the problem, Keith thought, because he didn't know anything about that kind of stuff. "Sir," he responded.

Sprague explained, "We need you to make us a sail."

"A really big sail," Reynolds added.

Keith shifted his weight as he tried to figure out the proper response. "Sir?" he said again. They wanted him to make a what?

Sprague explained the concept. "I know what this sounds like, believe me, but the idea is that if we can close off . . ." He paused and picked up Reynolds's sketch to illustrate his point. "Here. Look. The fo'c'sle's like a wind tunnel. The wind gets in there and blows us around. If we close it off, we're pretty sure we can compensate for the jammed rudder."

Keith took the sketch and looked at it. The concept sort of made sense. Back in high school, he'd ridden in an old Ford convertible as a prince in his class king and queen's entourage, and the wind had literally blown the crown off the queen's head. But when it started raining on the parade and they had put the top up, it was nice and calm inside.

There was really only one problem with Sprague's request. Despite being the sailmaker, he had never made a sail. There is no use for a sail on an aircraft carrier. Everybody knew that. Hatch covers, those body bags, but a sail? He inhaled, then said what was on his mind. "Sir, I don't know. I've never done anything like that before."

"None of us have, Boats," Sprague admitted with a wry chuckle. "But it's not the kind of sail you're imagining, one of those big things the old sailing ships used. Like the ones you've seen in the movies. Think of it more like a long, big sheet. How long do you think something like that might take you?"

Keith noted that the captain did not ask *if* he could do it, just how fast. *Well*, he thought, *I guess I do have a little bit of training.* He'd been taught the rudiments of sailmaking in the sewing courses he took in the two-week sailmaker's school in Philadelphia. And he was pretty sure he had seen some instructional guides in one of the storage lockers in the workshop. "I don't know, Sir," he responded, but even as he did, he had begun calculating exactly what he would need to get it done. If it had to be done, he would make the effort. That was his job. But he had no idea what they were looking for. "How large do you need it to be?"

Sprague looked at Johnson for the answer. The chief threw up his hands. "We're not exactly sure yet. We'll get you the measurements." Imagining the area that a sail would have to cover, he added, "Figure a rectangle say, a couple hundred feet long by what?" He glanced at Reynolds. "Fifteen, twenty feet high maybe?"

"Let's get somebody down there right away to figure it out," Sprague said.

Keith considered it. If he had a lot of help . . . They weren't asking for a finished sail. Like the captain said, it was more like a big, strong sheet. It wasn't going to be pretty, that was for sure, but nobody cared what it looked like. He took an optimistic guess. "We can do it in a day. I think, maybe a little faster."

"Faster is better," Sprague replied. "We'll give you whatever you need."

"Yes, Sir." As he hustled back to the workshop, his mind was racing. In his whole life, this was by far the most important thing he had ever been asked to do. Up until then, the biggest responsibility he had ever had was making sure there was enough punch, Coke, and ice at the senior prom committee. By nature, he played a supporting role in life. There was a reason he played tackle, blocking for the real stars, rather than running back. He was comfortable in the background.

The captain didn't exactly say the survival of the ship depended on him, but boy, that certainly was the impression they gave.

The good news was that the sail would be made of canvas, and he had plenty of canvas onboard to work with. The United States Navy had made certain of that. For a while, providing sufficient canvas had been a serious problem. Canvas was made from hemp, a fast-growing plant known for producing unusually strong fibers. It grew amazingly fast, too. Farmers around the world had grown it for centuries. They would throw down some seed and within weeks have a 16-foot plant. It was grown in every British colony. The Pilgrims brought hemp seeds with them to the new world. George Washington and Thomas Jefferson grew fields of hemp; in some places, farmers were permitted to pay taxes with it. The Conestoga wagons that settled the West were covered with it.

Hemp fibers were easy to wind into ropes and weave into canvas. The result was a strong, durable, water-resistant product. The American military had been using it since Revolutionary days for everything from tents to ship's ropes. It had required 120,000 pounds of hemp fiber just to make the ropes and sails for Old Ironsides, the USS *Constitution*.

Canvas was considered the ultimate utility fabric. In an emergency, it could be used for almost any purpose. *Bismarck's* crew had stuffed canvas in the holes in its hull to try to stop the flooding.

For a period in the late 1930s, there had been a shortage of hemp in the United States. The reason for that was political:

another by-product of the plant is cannabis. Marijuana. And that had created a problem. After the repeal of Prohibition the 4,000 agents of the federal government's Bureau of Prohibition, which had been policing alcohol, had little to do. To keep this army of revenuers in business, in 1937 the government declared marijuana an illegal narcotic. Farmers stopped growing it, forcing the government to become dependent on imported hemp, mostly from the Philippines and the East Indian subcontinent.

By 1940, Japan had severed those supply lines, causing a dangerous shortage. The Navy in particular was desperate for it. In response, the Roosevelt administration had launched a Hemp for Victory campaign, urging farmers to prove their patriotism by planting fields of hemp. Instructional films were made showing farmers how to plant it and reap the crop. Forty-two hemp mills were opened to process it. In Wisconsin, to compensate for the labor shortage created by the draft, German POWs were put to work in those mills.

The campaign worked. By the time *Intrepid* was launched, the hemp industry was fulfilling the military's needs.

"Flash" Gordon began his sewing project by spreading the word. He needed some help. He was pretty certain that among the ship's 3,000-man crew, there had to be at least a few people who knew something about sails or had sewing skills. He just needed a few of them.

Initially, much of the crew thought it was a bad joke. They were all concerned about the jammed rudder, but they were confident their officers would figure out some solution. Something technological, the kind of stuff the brass had been taught at Annapolis that was above their pay grade. As much as possible, they just went about doing their jobs. So when they heard a rumor that the captain wanted them to make a sail, they didn't believe it. "What does he think we're going to do, sail this ship back to Pearl?"

Another rumor claimed that the radar shack had been warned to keep a lookout for pirate ships appearing on the horizon.

Slowly, the word spread that this sailmaking wasn't a joke. The captain actually intended to raise a sail and steer the ship home with it. Most of the crew didn't understand the concept; they visualized Errol Flynn's popular *Captain Blood*, in which the ship was propelled by numerous white sails billowing in the wind.

It was impossible to imagine *Intrepid* flying those big sails.

It created serious anxiety. It didn't make a lot of sense. When they had moved the planes forward and flooded the stern, they sort of understood the reason: redistributing the weight changed the profile of the ship in the water. It made it lower, diminishing the impact of the wind. The captain knew what he was doing. But a sail?

Until that moment, few of them had realized the situation was desperate enough to require a crazy solution. The fact they had to resort to something as wild as this . . . this . . . they didn't know how to describe it, but it meant that they had run out of proven solutions. The news shook up a lot of people. Everybody on board knew the story of *Bismarck*, how its jammed rudder had led directly to the British sinking her.

Somewhere, deep in their minds, they identified with *Bismarck*'s crew. They would do whatever it took to avoid that fate.

More than a dozen men reported to Keith's workshop. They brought a wide range of sailing experience. A couple of them had crewed on oceangoing yachts. Several others owned small sailboats of their own, and one aircraft mechanic actually had been a sewing machine repairman in a Massachusetts mill before enlisting. He knew those Singers well. "You treat 'em right," he always said, "they'll treat you right."

In days of yore, warships had gone to sea carrying dozens of bolts of canvas 39 yards long and 2 feet wide, of varying thickness. That no longer was necessary as modern ships were easily resupplied, and no one had supposed they would suddenly need a thousand yards or more of canvas. *Intrepid* carried several rolls in the storeroom but not nearly enough to make a sail of the size that was necessary.

So once again, he put word on the grapevine: canvas. *We need canvas. As much canvas as you can find. Take it from anywhere and everywhere where it isn't essential.* Canvas was ubiquitous on the ship, the do-everything waterproof fabric. It was used for tarps to cover lifeboats, planes, and guns; it was used for hammocks, for hatch covers, officers' shower curtains, ordinary seabags, and, of course, body bags.

Even though the crew didn't understand the reason for it, they embraced the job. Doing something, even busy work, felt a whole lot better than doing nothing. It allowed them to forget that Japanese subs were out there, hunting for them. So, given a task, they went to work.

They began stripping *Intrepid* of its canvas. Back home, many of them had participated in the various collection drives, from bits of foil to be used as chaff to fool enemy radar to old 78-rpm records that were melted down for the shellac

needed to churn out new records. They knew what to do.
The crew embraced the challenge, competing to see which
department could supply the most canvas. Bets were placed.
Lockers were emptied; seabags that men had carried through
a dozen stations were tossed on a growing pile. In several instances, fights had to be broken up as men fought over a large
piece. Guards had to be stationed to protect canvas that could
not be spared—canvas life rafts, for example.

Within hours, they had collected far more canvas than
turned out to be necessary, but that made little difference
in the spirit it had aroused. They had been assigned a task,
and they delivered the Navy way. The *Intrepid* way. Captain
Sprague's way. Every member of the crew was now personally invested in this scheme.

While this was taking place, Sprague and Reynolds, Rick
Gaines, and their officers continued their struggle to maintain control of the ship. The battleship escorts were standing
by a few thousand yards away on either side, but there was
little assistance they could offer. Keeping the port engines at
full power pushed the ship forward in a helter-skelter pattern; Reynolds described the course as "a seismograph reading gone wild."

Sprague was exhausted. They all were. That was a fact of
life at sea in combat. There always was something more to
be done; there always were too few hours to do it. In addition to his other responsibilities, Sprague had to deal with
the mandatory paperwork. The Navy wanted every decision
recorded. Not so much why, but what. Facts, not opinion.
The torpedo hit the ship exactly when? How many men were
buried at sea? When did you change course? So as he sat at

his desk, writing this report, he paused to consider how to describe his decision to construct a sail. On paper, without an explanation, it would seem ridiculous: *ordered a sail constructed and rigged*. Instead, he wrote simply and as generally as possible, "Unable to repair jammed rudder. Control of the ship erratic. Instituted emergency measures."

And as he wrote those words, he had to face his own doubts. A captain doesn't have the luxury of showing concern or indecision to the crew. The captain had to be resolute, firm, and confident in his decisions. A captain could not show weakness. But in the solitude of his cabin, he could face reality. He took a long, deep, reflective breath. Could this work? Yes, it could. Would it work? The only way of finding out was to do it. If there was anything else, anything based on experience, that offered a better chance of success, he certainly would have pursued that. But there wasn't.

There was one other task he had to do. He took a sheet of paper from his desk drawer and began writing. "Dear Evie," he began, once again defaulting to his optimism. He tried to write home several times a week and focused on being upbeat. Besides, wartime censorship rules had to be respected. "We were in a scrap but got out with a few scratches. You should see the other guy! It is a moonless night in a great ocean, and the beauty of the moment never escapes me . . ."

Not precisely accurate, but he knew it would make her smile. In fact, the weather remained February-rough; 20- to 30-knot winds continued pushing the ship. The only good thing about it was that the persistent cloud cover offered at least a minimum of protection. Enemy planes were up there, scouring the ocean for the task force. If those planes or submarines spotted them, there was little they could do to escape. They couldn't maneuver, and without being able to turn into the wind, they could launch only a very limited number of planes from the catapults.

Once again, survival was a matter of luck.

Just after 2100 on the night of February 21, radar picked up a bogey circling 20 miles to port, as if it had spotted something and was investigating. Sprague was called to the radar room; he stood behind Ray Stone, a calming hand resting on Stone's shoulder as they silently watched the plane. There was no way of determining what they were wondering: *ours or theirs?*

Finally, the pilot seemed satisfied, and the plane disappeared from the screen. It had not been identified. Sprague tapped Stone on the shoulder twice—*good job*—and left without a word.

While this was going on, work crews in the fo'c'sle were measuring the space that would be enclosed by the sail and figuring out how to rig it. In port on a calm day, this would not have been challenging. It just required being careful and paying attention. But in choppy seas on a meandering ship, with winds howling and waves kicking up, it was wet, difficult, and dangerous.

Dick Montfort was a leader of that effort. It was far more complicated than just stretching a big sheet over open space. Reynolds had assigned him to the task because he admired his analytical mind—and his mechanical ability. Since the ship had been christened, Montfort had stayed busy solving problems, keeping the generators running, magically threading wires through bulkheads, making emergency repairs after the attack to keep the ship running. Years of figuring out how to safely bring safe, modern wiring to aging New York City buildings for ConEd had given him a lot of experience handling unique situations.

And as Montfort thought, "unique" didn't begin to describe this one. This was a different kind of problem. But like the captain, he loved solving intriguing challenges. He was good at it. When Reynolds had described the concept to him, Montfort asked for details. Reynolds almost laughed. "Whatever works. Is that good enough?"

Like any good engineer, Montfort began by surveying the job. Getting a general impression of exactly what he was dealing with. The fo'c'sle was a wide-open gap. He guessed it was more than 100 feet across and at least 20 feet high. It certainly could have been bigger. It looked to be pretty straight from side to side to him. A sail, a properly rigged sheet, would cover most of it. But, he noted, there was an additional problem no one had mentioned to him. There was a second smaller open area on the right, separated from the main gap by structural beams and sharply angled to starboard. That also had to be closed, or the winds would continue sweeping through that space. He made his notes. He had an idea how to deal with that. Then he went back to the captain's question: *How we gonna rig this thing?*

There were several grips and holds that could be used to tie it down. There also was a large cargo net that was used to lift materials aboard the ship, but on occasion was stretched across the opening as a safety measure when the deck was unusually wet. In fact, during a storm only a few weeks earlier a sailor had lost his balance and slid into the net, saving his life. After that the basketball players in his section began referring to him as "Two points." There also were two large capstans, windlasses used to raise and lower the massive anchor chains. Nobody had told him the sail had to be adjustable, but that possibility intrigued him.

He had to make a lot of decisions with only a limited amount of information: where to hang it, how to tie it down, what they would need to adjust it. *If* they would need to adjust it. He knew it would have to be *jury-rigged*, an ancient seagoing term describing an improvised sail. And if ever a sail was improvised, this was it. For Montfort, it was never a question of *if* it could be rigged—whatever it took, he would get it done—but first he had to solve the how.

He was busy taking measurements and roughing a few sketches when Phil Reynolds showed up with a young sailor. Montfort was chewing on the stem of his cherrywood pipe, although the bowl was turned upside down and empty. The smoking lamp was definitely out in every open area, but the stem still provided a scent of comfort.

"Chief," Reynolds introduced him, "this is Bosun Keith. He's the man who is gonna make this thing for us. Captain wanted him to see what we're talking about." Reynolds had to shout to be heard.

Keith had never been in the fo'c'sle area either. It was like being in the ship's open mouth. Within a few seconds, he knew what the captain was talking about: a swirling gust of wind almost ripped his helmet right off his head. He had to grab it and hold on to it as they spoke. A cold, irritating spray, too—colder even than the creek back home—was blowing right in his face. Reynolds left the two of them there, reminding Keith to let him know what he needed.

With a wave of his hand, Montfort encompassed the opening. "We'll get you ballpark dimensions." He then began
describing how it might be rigged.

Keith listened respectfully. He was getting comfortable
with all that responsibility he had been handed. He was much
younger than the captain, Commander Reynolds, and Chief
Montfort, but they all treated him with respect. They didn't
care how young he was, they expected him to do the job. That
was the Navy way, where rank and experience mattered, not
age. But still, he couldn't help paying deference to his elders;
that's the way he had been growed up.

His jeans and work shirt were still damp when he got back
to his workshop, so he turned off the industrial fan. With no
ventilation, it got warm enough to quickly dry him off. While
he was gone, a small mountain of canvas had been left outside
his workshop. Historically, sailmaking had been an art. Sails
were cut to fit a specific mast. They were wider at the foot
than at the head; extra material was included in the middle,
called the bunt, which allowed the sail to fill with wind and
billow out. Different grades of canvas were selected and sewn
together to make the sail lighter in the center and stronger
at the edges to deal with increased strain. The edges were
doubled over, and cord was stitched along the edge. These
sailmakers used waxed twine to hold various pieces together,
and it was accepted that a zigzag stitch, up and down, up and
down, was far superior to a traditional straight stitch because
it added strength and flexibility to the seams. It was a tedious
process, and it could take as long as a thousand man-hours to
make a topsail for a 74-gun ship.

Almost none of that mattered to Keith. His assignment was
simple: get it done. Now. Quickly. *We need it yesterday!* Nobody

cared what it looked like. It only had to be strong enough to last a few days. If the great sailmakers were like Rembrandt, Keith knew, he was more like that guy Picasso, the Spaniard whose paintings didn't look much like real paintings—people were still trying to figure out what his big mural called *Guernica* was supposed to be—because this sail sure wasn't going to look like the standard image of a sail.

Traditionally, as Keith had just learned from the copy of Robert Kipping's classic *The Elements of Sailmaking* he'd found in the storage room, when constructing a sail, individual pieces of canvas would be laid down on the floor of the sail loft until the entire sail was outlined. Then each piece would be numbered and cut to fit. He had neither the time nor space to do that, as the constant flow of messages from Reynolds—*How are you doing? Do you need anything? Can we help? How soon will this be done?*—reminded him.

The canvas workshop had been squeezed into the available space on the third deck as if it were an afterthought. It was wedged between a gas induction passage, catapult machinery, and a storage room. The compartment itself was sufficiently large but irregularly shaped. Rather than four straight walls, bulkheads had been constructed in front of the ship's operating machinery. Walls jutted in and out seemingly without any reason: certain walls were 4 feet long or 5 feet, then suddenly recessed 2 feet, then extended another 8 feet. In places the ceiling dropped several feet, which created alcoves. Two enclosed ammunition hoists, resembling elongated student's lockers, ran diagonally across the workshop from the floor through the ceiling, and were used to transport the 55-pound 5-inch/.38 caliber shells from the handling and projectile stowage to the gun tubs. Not an inch of space was wasted: pipes lined every wall, fire hoses were folded against the ceiling, and metal shelves had been cut to fit into every niche. The two large worktables in the room were made by resting 2-inch-thick wooden planks on metal frames. The ship's two Singer Zig Zags sat on those tables. Everything a sailmaker might need, from different strength needles to a variety of threads and even a box of thimbles, was on the shelves.

Keith gathered his makeshift crew around his sewing machine for a quick tutorial. "Okay," he began, feeling surprisingly confident, "here's how we're gonna get this done." We'll start by picking out those pieces with longest, straightest edges, he told them. Three men were assigned to select sheets. They passed them to cutters, who cut them into rough rectangles. Keith took his position behind the Singer. He was going to stay there for a long time.

He began by hemming the pieces he would use at the top and bottom of the sail, folding the canvas over about 4 inches, creating a channel for the rope that could hold up the sail. Chief Montfort didn't know for sure how it was going to be rigged, but whatever he did, Keith knew strong ropes would be needed to hold it in position.

As Kipping had advised, rather than the straight stitch, he used the stronger zigzag stitch. Coincidentally, that was his mother's go-to stitch. "It's supposed to look like a mountain chain," he explained to his crew, running his finger over the up-and-down pattern. Then he frowned at that suggestion and decided, "Maybe think of it like a row of dunce caps."

Then he began sewing sheets of canvas together; this was more like making a quilt than a sail, he decided. And he definitely knew how to do that. Every bed in the house was covered with a beautiful quilt handmade by his mother.

The crew created an assembly line. Pickers handed sheets of canvas to the cutters, who gave them to the feeders—two men facing each other across the worktable—who fed them to Keith. Dozens of individual sheets of canvas had to be sewed together to form strips several feet wide and almost 30 feet long. Then those strips would be sewed together lengthwise, sort of like sewing the stripes in an American flag. The shop had not been designed to make anything near this size, so they had to figure it out and make the necessary adjustments as the work progressed. For example, two men sat cross-legged under the table to hold up the folded cloth and keep it moving so Keith could continue sewing. Two other sailors, the pullers, stood on the other side of the machine, pulling the now bound pieces until they were free of the table and letting the cloth fold naturally into a pile.

The rhythmic pounding of the machine briefly lulled Keith into the warmth of nostalgia. While his industrial machine made a deeper, more defined thumping sound than the faster, lighter pat-pat-patter of his mother's home model, for a few brief seconds, it brought him back to those late afternoons when he sat under the vibrating wooden sewing table while his mother made necessary repairs and alterations.

They worked through the night. The shop grew hot and uncomfortable. The fans helped a bit, but more people were crammed into the compartment than had ever been intended. Several men had taken off their shirts, and beads of sweat rolled down their backs. The sewing wasn't difficult. Singer made a quality machine.

There was little conversation in the workshop beyond "Do you really think this thing is going to work?" That was the question for which there was no answer. Keith was noncommittal. "Well, the Captain thinks so and he knows a lot more about this stuff than I do. Let's just get it done, then we'll see."

"Tell you one thing," one of the cutters said. "This is gonna make a helluva story one day." He added with typical doomsday humor, "Assuming we make it, that is."

Twice during the night, Frank Johnson personally stopped by to make sure they had everything they needed, offering to get coffee or bring in some new men. But Keith understood this was just a subtle way of pushing them to work faster.

While a sail was being created out of bits and pieces, Sprague remained in contact with the destroyer escorts. They wanted to know what he was doing and how they might assist him. He was reluctant to provide any details. It wasn't only a sensible fear of broadcasting the ship's vulnerability, on the small chance the enemy might be listening. He also didn't quite know how to explain that he was making a sail and intended to use it to buffer the winds.

The sail slowly took shape, although no one in Keith's crew could accurately describe its shape: sort of like a rectangle but not exactly. Or, think of a big square, then forget that because it definitely was not square.

They finished just as the sun was rising. No one knew precisely how big it was, but in his official reports, Sprague reported it was 3,000 square feet. That was a guess. It was far too large to spread out in the compartment to measure. They couldn't even estimate how much it weighed. Maybe

400 pounds? 500? It easily could have been more. But it was big, bulky, and heavy.

There was a brief discussion about naming it; there was a Navy tradition of assigning nicknames to equipment. The inflatable life vest, for example, was widely known as a Mae West in tribute to that movie star's legendary figure. A couple of Keith's crew suggested the sail be referred to as the Rita to honor pinup star Rita Hayworth's impressive measurements. But beyond a few salacious snickers, it just didn't catch on. It was "the sail," "the thing," or on occasion, "Sprague's sail."

Getting it to the fo'c'sle through the narrow passageways, numerous hatches, and up ladders proved to be considerably more of a challenge than anyone had anticipated. As tired as they were, each of them hoisted a section and began carrying it through the ship. They had to carry it, push it, drag it, pull it. All along the route, men popped out of compartments to get a look at it or give some assistance. Frank Johnson later compared it to the Chinese New Year parade he had seen in San Francisco, in which dozens of men inside a dragon costume weaved through the narrow streets of Chinatown.

A swarm of carpenters was already at work when they finally got there. Montfort had solved the issue of the open space on the starboard side in typical ConEd fashion: if you can't fix it, board it up. He wouldn't even estimate how many doors and windows in aging buildings he had ordered sealed until potentially dangerous violations could be corrected. The same solution would work in this relatively small space. Board it up. Put up a wind barrier. Carpenters were busy erecting a wooden wall; three lengths of timber stretched horizontally across the opening were holding plywood sheets in place.

Sprague and Gaines were waiting in the forecastle with more men to hang it, most of them wearing foul weather gear. None of them had had any idea what the finished sail would look like, but they were disappointed. "That's it?" one of them said. "Wow."

They looked to Sprague for guidance. He was doing his best to convey confidence, but the reality of the pile of canvas in front of him made that difficult. "Great job, men," he told Keith's crew with as much enthusiasm as he could generate, then went down the line, shaking each man's hand. Finally, he turned to his crew and said the historic words he had never heard said in his career: "Okay, men. Let's hoist the sail."

EIGHT

TOM SPRAGUE HAD read David Porter's extraordinary journals during his freshman year at Annapolis. Porter had been master commandant of the first *Essex*, a 36-gun frigate during the War of 1812. As he later confessed, he had violated orders and sailed 2,500 miles around Cape Horn—the frigate barely surviving a massive storm—to become the first American warship to enter the Pacific Ocean.

His description of that storm had stayed with Sprague: "An enormous wave broke over the ship, and for an instant destroyed every hope," Porter wrote. "Our gun-deck ports were burst in, both boats on the quarters stove; our spare spars washed from the chains; our head-rails washed away . . . and the ship perfectly deluged and water logged . . . the immense torrent of water that was rushing down the hatchways . . . many who were washed from the spar to the gun-deck, and from their hammocks and did not know the extent of the damage, were also greatly alarmed; but the men at the wheel, and some others, who were enabled by a good grasp to keep their stations, distinguished themselves by their coolness and activity . . ."

Although Sprague had never said it aloud, that's what he had always strived to be: the man at the wheel.

In his own career, he had been through more terrible storms than he cared to remember. His ships had been bruised and battered. There had been moments after being smashed by a wave that he'd held his breath until the ship righted itself. On occasion, when the situation was stressful, he would remind himself it was not nearly as bad as David Porter being swamped in the Pacific.

He slapped his gloved hands together, more for warmth than for attention. Conditions on *Intrepid*'s fo'c'sle were miserable. The crew assembled by Montfort and Johnson to hang the sail was wet and cold. *Well*, Sprague said to himself, looking out at the roiling Pacific through the open end of the ship, *it's definitely not as bad as Porter's situation.* "Okay, gentlemen," he said, "let's get to it."

The question was how to rig it. As nothing like this had ever been done before, there was no model to follow. It was all best guess and hope it worked. Montfort and Frank Johnson had roughed out a plan. The two men had spent months exploring the ship; they generally knew every hook and nook, every handhold, rope, and railing, every shelf, cranny, and locker—and its purpose. Everything on the ship was functional, put there to fulfill a need. There were no esthetic enhancements. It didn't matter what it looked like. *Intrepid* was a warship built at great cost for one purpose only: destroy the enemy.

Sprague and Reynolds made a couple of suggestions. Then the captain approved it.

Johnson had put a 27-man crew together to implement it. They began by collecting spare rope and cord. Thanks to

Hemp for Victory, there was no shortage of that aboard. As soon as the sail was delivered, several men began threading a heavy rope through both the top and bottom channels, using a simple bowline to knot pieces together.

The weather complicated the task. Sailors were used to working in bad weather. They considered it part of the job description. For some men, their resilience was a source of pride. But working in this exposed area, where the deck was often wet and slippery and the winds met to play their tricks, was unusually precarious.

Johnson's crew stretched out that netting on the deck, then laid the sail on top of it. This was the first time the sail had been completely unrolled. They took a step back to look at it. It was big. That was obvious. It actually was substantially longer and wider than the net. Open to its full length, with its multishades of gray and white canvas, it most resembled a plasterers used floor tarp.

"Okay," Johnson shouted, "here we go." He had to shout to be heard over the banging of the ship's carpenters finishing Montfort's wall. With the sail still lying on the deck, they tossed lines around the overhead beams on the bottom of the flight deck, as if hanging a shower curtain, then threaded them through the O-rings running the length of the sail. They left considerable slack in the lines. One thing every sailor was good at was running lines and tying knots. Ordinary seamen essentially were naval roustabouts, capable of raising a circus tent on the village green or a sail in a stormy sea.

When they were done, eight ropes ran through O-rings the length of the sail and over beams. Three or four men took hold of each rope. On Johnson's command, "Heave," they began pulling the ropes, slowly raising the sail in place.

"Heave." In olden days, they might have been chanting. Gradually, the top of the sail lifted off the deck. "Heave." It was raised several inches, as much as a foot, with each command. "Heave." The higher it went, the heavier it got. "Heave!" As they raised the canvas sheet, wind gusts tested it, threatening to rip it off the rings. "Heave!"

One of the men, "Fitzie" Fitzgerald, later said it made him think of the curtain in his high school auditorium going up— and that never worked smoothly either. "Heave."

The ocean spray added to its weight. Even in the Pacific cold, several men were sweating. When the sail finally was lifted completely off the deck, the wind caught the bottom; it started fluttering, making it even more difficult to manage. Almost instantly, several men slid underneath and grabbed the bottom, holding it in place.

Once the sail was entirely off the ground, Johnson directed them, "Okay! Okay! Tie it down. Tie it down."

They tied the ropes to any fixture they could find, once again leaving considerable slack in the ropes. But rather than the sail being lashed to the deck to secure it in position, the ropes extending from the top and bottom were tied to the anchor chains that rotated around the capstans. That was Montfort's concept. On the ships of yore, sails were rigged to be put up, taken down, moved, or adjusted very quickly. The fate of the ship depended on it. Attaching those ropes to the electrical capstans made it possible to adjust the tension of the sail. Theoretically, it could be tightened or given slack. It actually could be moved a few feet from side to side to respond to changes in the wind's direction.

Additionally, Johnson's men tied it to the beams with a variety of knots, a combination of loops, hitches, and stoppers. If it caused any serious unexpected problems, he could simply cut the ropes and let the whole thing blow away.

Throughout the ship, the scuttlebutt was running full speed ahead: *They got that thing to the fo'c'sle. They're trying to put it up. They're having trouble figuring out the wind.* And the rumors: *It's too big. It's too small. Wind's just ripping it apart.*

Those men who had seen the sail tried to describe it to their shipmates, especially those men who assumed the sail was going to look like a sail: *imagine the biggest Band-Aid you've ever seen.* Or, *it's like the Jolly Green Giant's handkerchief.* Or, *it's a giant wind sock.* Many of them illustrated the width of the sail by stretching out their arms as far as possible. It was big. That was the point.

When it was finally in place, the cargo net was stretched behind it, anchored with ropes to hooks and beams. Then the sail was tied to the net in several places to provide some sort of stability.

The sail—and Montfort's wooden wall—had been devised, created, and pulled, pushed, and hammered into position in less than one day. It was a marvelous feat, a tribute to the teamwork that Sprague had instilled. There was only one last question to answer: Would it work?

And, as always, bets were placed: *It's gonna save the ship. It's a joke.*

While the sail was being raised, Sprague joined Reynolds, Gaines, Tom Wallace, and several other men on the bridge. Tom Sprague was a realist. Even if this didn't solve the problem, it might provide some assistance. If it didn't

The sail of *Intrepid*. *Collection of the Intrepid Museum. P00.2012.01.27*

work, there was no backup plan. They would continue sla-
loming towards Hawaii—but that still was almost 2,500 miles
away. If they couldn't make it, they would take whatever safe
harbor they could reach, anyplace emergency repairs could
be made.

From there? As he knew, ancient maps supposedly identified unexplored regions with the Latin words *hic sunt dracones*: here be dragons. They were in *hic sunt dracones* territory.

"It's up," he told Reynolds. "Let's see what it does." The
starboard engines had been running at full power to compensate for the jammed rudder. Sprague told the helmsman,
"Reduce revolutions on the starboard shafts to one third."

"Starboard engine reduced one third."

They waited.

A small group gathered on the fo'c'sle to see if this thing worked, although no one knew what to expect. Johnson and his crew had remained there, making sure the sail was secure, that the wind didn't simply rip it from its moorings. The winds tested it, shifting to put pressure on various points. They could see the ropes straining to hold it in place. It held.

There was little conversation on the bridge. As every carrier pilot has experienced, the instant after leaving the flight deck, the plane dips down toward the water before the winds lift the wings. It's a terrifying feeling. Carrier pilots, especially in Sprague's early years, used to joke, "Don't fly if you can't swim." No matter how many times he had taken off from a deck, that feeling never went away. Butterflies, as some people referred to it. Until gravity caught the plane, the thought flashed through the pilot's mind: *this could be the last time.*

Sprague had that same queasy feeling in the pit of his stomach as he waited on the bridge. Seconds passed. He glanced at the Bendix Friez wind indicator. Its arrow remained steady from port at 22 mph. Reynolds was standing next to him. He said softly, "Maybe?"

Sprague nodded. Reducing the engines should have caused the prevailing winds to push the bow farther to starboard. That didn't seem to be happening. That was a hopeful sign. But only after the winds shifted direction or gained or even reduced force would they be able to fully gauge the effect of the sail.

On the fo'c'sle, Frank Johnson was continuously in motion, yanking on lines, inspecting knots. It was busy work, a means to expend the bolts of energy surging through his body. He needed to do something, and there was nothing else to do. "What do you think, Chief?" one of his men asked.

Johnson tugged on one of the overhead lines. "She's good," he replied, nodding.

"No. I mean you think it's going to work?"

"It's a big sheet of canvas," he said noncommittally. The real answer was, he didn't have the slightest idea. After decades in the Navy, he'd seen or experienced pretty much everything you can imagine; he was running out of firsts. But this? This definitely was a first.

He trusted Sprague and Reynolds, though. Gaines, too. They were good people. They seemed to know what they were doing.

And then the winds shifted.

Sprague had been staring at the wind indicator. Waiting. As he watched, it seemed to flicker. If he hadn't spent so many years reading the wind, he might not even have noticed it. With a slight nod, he directed Reynolds's attention to it. "Here we go."

"Yeah, I saw."

The wind had picked up slightly, to about 18 knots, but more telling, its direction had shifted closer to true east. According to the gyro, though, the ship barely responded. The sail appeared to be blunting the effect of the wind. "Starboard engines all ahead full," Sprague ordered hopefully.

As the starboard engines came up to full power, *Intrepid* remained mostly on the desired course. The abrupt wrenching from side to side had not been eliminated, but it had been greatly reduced. Sprague took a long, deep, satisfying breath and said to Reynolds, "Well, it's doing something."

Keith had led his team up to the hangar deck to see what their sail looked like fully extended and tied in position. It was disappointing. "That's it?" one of his men asked.

"Yep. That's it," Keith replied.

There wasn't really much to see, a long strip of canvas covering an open space, tied in all different places to various protrusions. They stood there looking at it for a few minutes as the sail fought the wind—and seemed to be winning. Their sail wasn't pretty, it wasn't going to win any prizes at somebody's county fair, but it was doing the job. Keith was satisfied with their work; the thing was holding together, and there weren't any obvious holes or openings in the seams.

They went back to the workshop, which was littered with bits and pieces of discarded canvas. They kept a few larger pieces in case they had to make some patches and packed up the rest of it. Tony Zollo came down from the bridge and said, "Captain says to tell all of you, well done."

"Is it working?" Keith asked.

Zollo shrugged. "Maybe. Seems like it." He smiled. "Yeah, it is."

That was the general impression throughout the ship. There was no single moment when the situation was instantly reversed. The feeling was more like Sprague's deep sigh of relief. An immediate crisis seemed to have been averted. They had regained some control of the ship. The sudden, unexpected swerves that knocked men into the bulkheads had ended, and the side-to-side swaying was noticeably reduced. While they were no longer riding Coney Island's fabled Cyclone roller coaster, they still were on the smaller, less precarious Switchback Railway, literally the country's first real coaster, with its gentle hills.

The crew aboard the destroyer *Stembel* had watched with fascination as Johnson's team struggled to hang this, this, whatever it was, this big gray-white canvas over the fo'c'sle. They couldn't quite figure out what it was or what it was supposed to do. From almost a thousand yards away, it looked like they were putting a surgeon's mask over an open mouth. *Stembel*'s captain finally signaled for clarification, wondering, "*Intrepid*, are you in need of further assistance?"

Intrepid replied, "Haven't you ever seen a sailboat before?"

On the bridge, they were going through the learning curve, trying to get a feel for the ship under sail. There were no equations, no graphs, no tables, no formulas they could help them. The variable, the X factor, was the direction and strength of the wind, and there was no easy way to account for that. That left trial and error, navigating by feel; reduce speed, increase speed, balance the port and starboard engines. When it works, hold it there until it doesn't work.

For Sprague and Gaines, aviators who once had flown by the proverbial "seat of their pants,"—a phrase originally used to describe flying without instruments in heavy fog and determining whether you were right side up or upside down by the pressure on the parachute on your back—this brought back memories of putting control of your fate in your own hands.

After the starboard engines took hold, Sprague ordered, "Steady as she goes." Then he added, chuckling, "Well, we'll see about that."

The helmsmen gradually acquired a feel for the ship "under sail." During low gusts, they were able to maintain a speed of 18 to 20 knots. They had to stay "on their toes," ready to instantly respond to the changing winds by adjusting engine thrusts, but they were able to maintain a rough heading.

At various times during the next few days, minor adjustments were made in response to the shifting winds. Using Montfort's capstan system, the sail was pulled taut so it stood rigid against the wind, or was given some slack so it absorbed more of it.

The crew also adjusted to the situation. Initially, few men had taken it seriously, even after they found out Sprague was serious. Hoist a sail on an aircraft carrier? No friggin' way. A few men had tried to explain the theory, drawing simple diagrams that showed wind arrows coming from port hitting the ship and pushing it to starboard. Then explaining that the sail would blunt the wind effect.

That had been followed by anxiety: *What do we do if this thing doesn't work?* With the ship unable to conduct air operations, other than utilizing the catapults if the situation got desperate, there was a lot of time to scan the skies and worry. A lot of what-ifs and no answers.

Then embarrassment kicked in. These men believed the United States Navy and Marines was the greatest fighting force in the world—and the ship on which they sailed, the *Essex*-class carrier *Intrepid*, was the most up-to-date, most powerful weapon in history. It was the finest example of American ingenuity and excellence.

A sail? The carrier had to be saved by pieces of canvas sewed together? Geez. They didn't want to even think about the ridicule they were going to hear when this story got around: *What's next, you gonna row it home? Who's in command, Captain No Beard?*

But once it was in place and looked like it was working, they sure weren't being jerked back and forth as sharply or frequently, they began to accept the humor in the situation. Three men in different parts of the ship completely independently had begun wearing patches over one eye while others wondered what happened to their "bottom of rum."

And finally, they developed a sense of pride in the sail. It was an incredibly innovative solution to a complex problem. It was a good thing *Bismarck*'s captain hadn't thought of it; it might have saved his ship. The Navy had always taken pride in being able to adjust to the situation, any situation, and this was just another example of creative thinking under stress. As men got off duty, they would go to the fo'c'sle to see it for themselves. They knew this story was going to spread throughout the service, and they wanted to be able to tell people that it was their ship. They were there. They saw it or even helped carry it or rig it.

Sprague informed the brass in Pearl Harbor that *Intrepid* had regained "operational control" by taking "emergency measures." The closest Sprague came to revealing any details was reporting, "We are sailing to destination."

Once more, luck mattered. No one knew if the sail could withstand stronger winds, nor did they want to test it. Obviously, it had limits, but unless they ran into a gale, they would never know what those limits were. Sprague checked the weather forecast regularly and, admittedly, anxiously as the ship made its way to Pearl Harbor, although it wouldn't have made any difference. If there was a storm in their path, there was little that he could do to avoid it.

At one point, he caught himself just staring at several grayish clouds. He mused to Gaines, "You ever thought about how much of our careers has been determined by the weather?"

Rick Gaines was a Navy man, one of countless fliers and sailors who had spent years planning his day based on the morning cloud cover. "Pretty amazing, isn't it?"

"So? What do you think?"

Gaines looked out at the morning sky and took a reflective breath. "I think we're gonna be okay. I think." He added, "I hope."

As *Intrepid* sailed toward Pearl Harbor, chances of encountering Japanese aircraft decreased—although enemy submarines were still out there. Lookouts and radar operators kept a sharp watch. As much as possible, the ship remained locked down. On both February 20 and 21, the crew went to general quarters, more as a precautionary measure than in response to an unidentified blip.

While Sprague and Gaines learned from looking at the clouds at sunrise, Montfort got his information from the drumming of the engines. The extra stress on the engines had caused recurring technical issues, keeping him busy and frustrated. The numbers 3 and 4 shafts were running consistently at an impressive 170 to 180 rpms. Some residual water damage from the torpedo caused overloads, so power had to be shifted between generators. Some of the auxiliary pumps failed. He was performing a high-wire juggling act, managing to keep the engines, *his* engines as he thought of them, because he had kept them mostly online, running smoothly.

It was a long, erratic voyage back to Hawaii. On February 22, as a way of breaking the tension and rewarding the crew for a job well done, it was announced, "Now hear this. Now hear this. All lowly polliwogs lend an ear. The

Royal Party from the Domain of Neptunus Rex, including the Royal Baby is coming alongside. Prepare to welcome them onboard."

Weeks earlier, *Intrepid* had simultaneously crossed the Equator and the International Dateline. For at least 400 years, sailors had celebrated "crossing the line" with a ceremony in which "polliwogs," those who had not previously crossed the equator, were initiated into the Ancient Order of the Deep by "trusty shellbacks," men who had made the crossing. It was a respected naval tradition—which *Intrepid* had not been able to honor in January because the crew was preparing for battle.

Sprague decided it would be a great morale booster for the crew.

It isn't known when or where this tradition started. Some historians suspect ancient sailors created it to test the seafaring skills of young hands. But over time, it evolved into a boisterous no-holds-barred event. There are no uniform rites or requirements, although during the ceremony, rank is ignored and makeshift costumes—including those of the "Ladies of the Royal Court"—are worn. In the proceedings, lowly polliwogs—both officers and men—are accused of committing outrageous "crimes" such as wearing the wrong clothes, laughing at bad jokes, failing to share cigarettes, and almost anything else. As punishment, to be accepted into his realm by King Neptune, they are sentenced to perform or endure inventive and sometimes embarrassing tasks, pranks, gags, obstacles, and physical punishment.

In the past, this hazing had been known to be physically abusive. On occasion, men were beaten with boards or flogged with wet ropes, forced to run through the gauntlet, or even dragged alongside the boat.

Not on Tom Sprague's watch. King Neptune, his mop-topped queen and "her" court, many of them wearing diapers, "arrived" by lifeboat and were piped aboard. *Intrepid's* crew was so young that there were only about 200 shellbacks to initiate the 3,000 polliwogs. Most of the crew, including many officers, enthusiastically participated. Rick Gaines, for example, failed to produce his shellback card and willingly went through the entire initiation process again; in his case, that meant kissing the royal baby's grease-smeared stomach, getting greased himself, and serving as lookout using Coke bottles as binoculars. He was granted a minor reprieve; unlike most of the polliwogs, he was not compelled to crawl on hands and knees through the 100-foot-long tunnel of garbage while being sprayed with fire hoses, dance a waltz while dressed in skivvies, or wear a silly sign.

However, "Most officers got a good going over," wrote Dick Montfort. "Painted from head to waist with grease. Hair and face included. Also put in stocks and belted a couple of times. Me? I got my forehead painted and then ran the gauntlet with fire hose on rear end . . ."

Alcohol was consumed, as you might have guessed.

There were a few broken limbs, caused mainly by sailors slipping on the deck soaked by fire hoses and covered with grease, but at the end, everyone received a Trusty Shellback certificate attesting to the fact that they had crossed the equator and fulfilled all the required duties.

One question plagued them: Where had all those diapers come from?

Sprague had been right. This had been an extremely difficult voyage, from the elation of the victory at Truk to the terror of being torpedoed, from the grief at having to bury their shipmates to the anxiety of having to improvise a unique solution to the jammed rudder. This celebration had finally allowed the crew to celebrate life. For so many of them, who had seen shipmates killed, it made a difference.

They weren't home yet; it would require another full day of bouncing around the Pacific before they got to Hawaii.

As they got closer, Sprague sent a message to the commander of the battleship escorts: "Before parting company may I express my appreciation for the skillful assistance of the ships under your command and for your solicitous understanding and thoughtfulness for the welfare and safety of *Intrepid*. Until we meet again best luck and good hunting to all hands."

The commander replied, "Your kind message very much appreciated. It has been a privilege to be of assistance to a gallant ship and crew."

The captain of one of those ships also responded, "We in the screen admire your fighting spirit by which . . . you have kept your damaged ship moving. We feel with you the loss of those who contributed their lives . . ."

They finally reached Pearl Harbor, Oahu, on the morning of February 24, 1944. Pearl Harbor was the base for fleet operations in the Pacific and one of the busiest ports in the world. Dozens of ships sailed in and out every day for supplies, repairs, and a respite from the war. Work never stopped. The *Lexington*, which also had been torpedoed, had been there for several weeks and was almost ready to depart. But none of them had ever entered the harbor like *Intrepid*.

The makeshift sail on the forecastle, which helped *Intrepid* hold to a course, after a fashion, on her way back to Pearl Harbor. *Collection of the Intrepid Museum. P00.2012.01.27*

"I don't believe I ever saw a more beautiful morning," Jake Elefant wrote in his diary. "The water was very smooth." They were safe.

Phil Reynolds was standing with Sprague on the captain's bridge. As they approached the entrance to the harbor, the slightly embarrassed Reynolds said, as tactfully as possible, to the captain, "You know, that sail really is pretty rough looking. You think maybe we should take it down?"

Sprague turned to him with a big grin on his face and replied firmly, "Nothing doing!"

For security reasons, no one in Pearl Harbor knew anything about the sail. Sailors, dock workers, and civilians were so accustomed to seeing big warships arrive that they rarely paid attention to them. But this . . . this was different. They had never seen anything like it. The word rippled through the harbor that *Intrepid* was coming in—with a sail. Many people raced down to the water to see it for themselves. They watched with curiosity, disbelief, and enjoyment as *Intrepid* was led by tugs to its berth. This was something different. Within a few minutes, a legend was born as incredulous workers began referring to the ship as "the first square-rigged aircraft carrier in Navy history."

Intrepid tied up at 1300. Within minutes, Admiral Chester Nimitz, Commander in Chief of the US Pacific Fleet, and several aides arrived and came aboard, as curious as everyone else to learn the whole story—and anxious to see this crazy-quilt sail for themselves. Among the first suggestions Sprague made to the admiral during this visit, which he would put in writing and eventually would be adopted by naval architects, was that in the future, carrier fo'c'sles be enclosed.

Sprague and Frank Johnson personally conducted Nimitz's tour. Gordon Keith was brought up to meet the admiral, who congratulated him. "I heard you made your Singer sing," Nimitz said. No one cringed.

A day later, *Intrepid* sailed into Dry Dock #1. After the ropes and cables had been secured, Sprague finally—and somewhat reluctantly—gave the order, "Okay, let's take it down."

No one knew what to do with it. Several sailors cut pieces from it to keep as souvenirs. But before repairs began, *Intrepid*'s great sail was bundled up and discarded.

It took another full day to secure the massive ship in the dry dock, and after the water had been drained, the officers and crew got their first look at the extent of the damage. "We finally saw the hole made by the fish," wrote Elefant. "The rudder was half-gone and bent out of shape. Side of ship had a hole clear into the steering gear room . . . chunks of steel armor as big as your hand gouged out of the armor walls.

"They also found what was left of one of the Chiefs that was missing . . ."

Commander Reynolds stood on the dock staring at the mangled rudder. The damage was far more extensive than he had imagined. About half of it was missing. The remainder was twisted into a shape the Gaines described as "a huge potato chip."

Sprague was also surprised by the magnitude of the damage. Having read the intelligence reports about damage to *Bismarck*, which speculated the rudder had been twisted and caught in the propeller shaft, he had guessed he was dealing with a similar problem. Asked later whether he would have done something differently if he had known the scope of the damage, he chuckled, shook his head, and replied, "There wasn't anything different."

Sprague also immediately went to work writing down everything he remembered. He would have to file a full report of the incident and wanted to make certain he included every detail. "The net result [of the torpedo]," he wrote, "insofar as ship control was concerned was to create the permanent effect of approximately 6 1/2 degrees left rudder . . . On the following day orders were received to proceed via Majuro.

This necessitated taking the wind on the port bow and steering control of the vessel was lost."

It read so matter-of-factly; *steering control of the vessel was lost.* As if he had misplaced his glasses rather than losing control of a 40,000-ton behemoth carrying more than 3,000 men in the stormy Pacific.

His officious tone suggested that the predicament was little more than an interesting problem: "It was obvious that the ship needed some headsail and the problem was how to rig a jib or reduce the effect of the jammed left rudder . . . a jury sail was then rigged between the forecastle deck and the underside of the flight deck.

"A sail of approximately 3,000 square feet was improvised . . ." he wrote, perhaps exaggerating the actual size of the sail—but reinforcing the growing legend. "With the E#1 shaft locked, the planes forward and the sail rigged, it was found the ship could be adequately controlled with the engines."

As the story of the sail spread and grew into near mythical proportions—a 3,000-square-foot sail!—a steady stream of curious visitors showed up to see the damaged ship. That included the chief engineer of the *Indiana*, which was also in dry dock after being rammed by the *Washington*. He wanted to compare events.

Intrepid's damage was far too extensive to be repaired at Pearl Harbor. The ship would have to return to Hunter's Point in San Francisco, where an entirely new rudder assembly could be fitted. How to get there became a contentious issue. Rather than trying to affix a temporary rudder, which Sprague believed necessary, technical personnel decided

Intrepid could make the trip through the relatively calm waters using its engine to steer.

No, Sprague argued, they couldn't. It made no sense; they had tried that. It didn't work in rough seas. How did they expect him to control a ship without a rudder? But he could not talk them out of it.

It took repair crews two full days working around the clock to remove the damaged rudder and patch the hole in the hull. On Leap Day, February 29, tugs pulled *Intrepid* into the ocean, released the lines, and wished her a safe voyage. In many cultures—Greece, Taiwan, and other places, for example—it is considered bad luck to begin anything, such as a marriage or a voyage, on Leap Day. That superstition almost immediately proved accurate.

The ship had made only a few miles when the winds picked up, as if they had been waiting patiently offshore for her to return to the ocean. "What a mess," reported Montfort. "Ship goes only in circles either one way or the other. Can't keep on course. Tried all kinds of ways to hold it. So we are going back into Pearl Harbor."

As Sprague later recorded, "The vessel sortied from Pearl in this condition and was found to be completely unmanageable . . . With the rudder completely removed it was found the hull had no directional stability whatsoever. The heading of the ship had no direct relation to the direction of the motion of the ship . . . At times the ship would swing uncontrollably through 360°."

As the ship spun completely out of control, several men asked themselves the obvious question: Why hadn't they saved the sail?

The winds toyed with *Intrepid* for several hours, then gradually decreased, allowing Sprague to regain a minimum of steering—but only at low speed. At 4 or 5 knots, he could keep the ship within a 15-degree arc. At his request, two seagoing tugs came out to haul *Intrepid* back into Pearl. But their attempts to attach lines to the ship in the Kona winds proved almost impossible. The first line, a 10-inch-thick hawser, suddenly snapped, whipping across the deck.

Carefully, slowly, the tug moved into position to make a second attempt. It got closer, closer, and then the wind drove it into *Intrepid*'s hull. Four life rafts ripped free, falling hard onto the tug. One deckhand barely avoided being hit by a raft. The rafts smashed windows and broke machinery on the tug.

It took several more attempts; one frustrated member of the tug's crew compared it to a cowboy trying to toss a lasso around a giant bronc on a roller coaster. But after several additional attempts, they managed to secure their towing wires.

And then they had to wait. The turbulent seas made it far too dangerous to try to tow the ship back into the harbor. *Intrepid* was ordered to stand several miles offshore until weather conditions improved. Its engines were shut down, and the tugs dragged it in circles at 3 or 4 knots to reduce the swinging.

For two days and nights, the ship was battered by the Pacific. With little else to do, Ray Stone remembered, like many of his crewmates, he listened to Japanese propagandist Tokyo Rose's nightly radio broadcast. Between playing records, Tokyo Rose, in an alluring voice, taunted Allied troops. On the second night, the crew was startled and slightly unnerved when she warned, "This next song is for those lonesome sailors on the carrier offshore Oahu. We know where you are and will send our submarines to sink you. Be sure to say your prayers before you close your eyes tonight."

Stone was stunned. The Japanese knew where they were. They knew they were in trouble. It was obvious enemy subs were out there, watching him, watching his ship. No one slept easily. Enemy submarines were always a threat, but this was more than that. This was a direct warning. The crew found some comfort in gallows humor. "Don't mean a damn thing," a bunkmate told Stone. "Even if they know we're here, they can't hit us. If we don't even know which way we're going, how are they gonna know?"

After the storm subsided, it took seven ships, including the tugs, the cruiser *Birmingham*, and three destroyer escorts, to corral *Intrepid* and bring her safely into the harbor.

While waiting for space in the dry dock, they tied up just behind the remains of the *Arizona*. More than two years had passed since it had been sunk, and bodies were still being taken out of the wreckage.

As Sprague had pleaded, over the next few days, a make-shift, hand-operated rudder was fastened to the hull. The primary piece, a rigid fin about the same size as the damaged rudder, was bolted in place. It could not be moved. But a second piece, a flipper, a moveable part about a quarter the size of the original rudder, was attached to it. It could only be moved right or left about 20 degrees, but engineers were confident this was enough to steer the ship.

Sprague was not quite so sure.

This flipper would be wired to a capstan on the fantail. Orders to turn the rudder would be given from the bridge to sailors stationed there, who would rotate the capstan. Once again, as in the days of sailing ships, *Intrepid* would literally be steered by hand.

Assuming it worked.

On March 16, the hole in the hull temporarily patched, the jury-rigged rudder in place, *Intrepid* was once again escorted out of Pearl Harbor. In the first hours at sea, Sprague gingerly tested the new rig, learning exactly how much steering control he had.

Some, was the answer.

Enough. The moveable flipper was intended to overcome the effect of the wind and currents, allowing Sprague to use the engines to steer. Well, he learned very quickly that didn't work. It didn't work at all. The engines simply weren't powerful enough to accomplish that. But through trial and error, he discovered that the exact opposite was true: the rudder worked! As he wrote, "The final combination, which proved very satisfactory, was to adjust engine revolutions to overcome the effect of the wind—and use the jury rudder to steer."

Under normal conditions, the voyage from Pearl Harbor to the West Coast of the United States took four days. This trip took a full week. The deck capstan had not been designed for continuous operation, so it had to be regularly cleaned and lubricated. Crews of men rotated through the days and night, some of them on the ropes, others oiling and swabbing. Like the sail, it was a reminder of the days when ships were run by men, not machines. It was a long, sometimes boring, but generally uneventful trip.

Until they reached San Francisco Bay.

Intrepid had performed efficiently, with adequate steering control at 14 to 16 knots in a calm ocean. Once more, Tom Sprague was the man at the wheel. But after entering San

Francisco Bay, the ship had to slow considerably. At those slower speeds, even in the calmer waters, even with tugs on either side of the ship, she became difficult to control. She started slipping. At lower speed, the small flipper had little effect. To compensate for that, *Intrepid* was scheduled to pass under the Golden Gate Bridge at full high tide, when currents are at a standstill, preparing to change direction.

Sprague maneuvered her into position precisely on time—but something was wrong. He checked all his instruments. The readings made no sense. "Captain," one of his junior officers said, "I've been checking the tide tables." He shook his head. "I don't know where we got these, but they're wrong. High tide was almost an hour ago."

"Let me see that, please." The young officer was right. The numbers did not square with what he was seeing. The tables were wrong. The tide was ebbing, which created powerful erratic currents. Currents far too strong for the crippled ship to navigate. Less than half a mile from the bridge, Sprague lost control of his ship. It started sliding left and right, left and right.

The bridge lay dead ahead.

Sprague responded coolly. After everything he had gone through, he was confident he could handle this. He began playing with his engines, putting the experiences of the last week into practice. In the calmer waters of the bay, he juggled the propellers to maintain control, deftly adjusting them to correct a sheer to the left or right.

They sailed safely under the bridge.

On March 16, Intrepid entered the dry dock at San Francisco Naval Shipyard at Hunter's Point.

They were home.

NINE

INTREPID DID WHAT?

The story of *Intrepid*'s incredible sail spread quickly throughout the Navy. Many sailors found it impossible to believe. An aircraft carrier rigging a sail? They were surprised when it turned out to be true. Tom Sprague's innovative solution had helped him save his ship—as strange as it sounded.

Sprague was honored for his actions. Securing *Intrepid* safely in dry dock turned out to be his last action as its captain. On March 22, while the ship was being repaired, Sprague was notified, "The President of the United States . . . appoints you a Rear Admiral in the Navy."

With that promotion came a new assignment. He was placed in command of Carrier Division 22, consisting of four escort carriers. Most of *Intrepid*'s crew was ashore on March 28, when a small group in dress blues assembled on the flight deck to watch him hand the ship over to Rick Gaines. It was a bittersweet moment. Since assuming command, Sprague had taken an untested sparkling new machine and given it a soul. He had transformed 3,000 individuals—the vast majority young and inexperienced—into a crew and led them into battle. And, as one crew member remarked, Sprague "was the one who brought us home."

"Those of us who have served on this latest *Intrepid* have no apologies to offer to those gallant men who first established the name in the list of fighting naval ships," Sprague said. "Brave officers and men paid with their lives as did those on the first *Intrepid* . . . We too assaulted the enemy in his strongholds, severely wounded him and withdrew but to strike another day . . ."

His words to his crew, his men, rippled through the crisp spring afternoon. "You have been halfway round the world and have proven yourselves." He praised the petty officers and warrant officers who brought "the young fellows along and welded them into an effective combat team . . ."

And he concluded, "Until we meet again, good hunting."

A long, loud cheer of appreciation filled the day. The official ceremony was followed several hours later by a party at which rank was ignored. Once again, alcohol was consumed.

While the Navy did not officially cite the creation of the sail as the reason, Admiral Thomas Sprague was awarded the Legion of Merit, which is given for "exceptionally meritorious conduct in the performance of outstanding services and achievements." The citation honored him for his remarkable leadership: "During the attack on Truk Atoll . . . [when] under the skillful leadership of Captain Sprague the damage was brought under control and the ship returned to a safe port under her own power."

"Under her own power" was as close as the Navy would ever come to acknowledging *Intrepid*'s sail.

Before leaving, Sprague made of point of issuing a letter of commendation to Commander Phil Reynolds for his "imperturbable skill, efficiency and personal courage . . . directing, coordinating . . . the work of restoring the *Intrepid* to a seaworthy condition . . ."

Frank Johnson and Gordon Keith were among the men commended for "contributing to the success of the mission." Fleet Commander Mitscher officially congratulated the entire crew on "a perfectly splendid job . . . [which] resulted in our first entry into the Japanese Empire after two years of tough opposition."

Gaines eventually handed command to Captain Joseph Francis Bolger. Bolger had followed Sprague's path; he was only a couple of years behind him at Annapolis and then at flight school in Pensacola. Like Sprague, Bolger was commanding a carrier for the first time, but he inherited a battle-tested crew.

The damage was even more severe than originally had been thought, and it took four months to make the necessary repairs. *Intrepid* finally sailed back into the war—with its new rudder and without its sail—in early June.

Captain Bolger was immediately tested. Incredibly, one day after leaving Pearl Harbor, gears in a propeller shaft failed— and *Intrepid* lost its steering.

Again.

While control was quickly regained, old fears resurfaced in now veteran crew members about the ship being cursed. While few men—if any—actually believed it, they couldn't deny it was an eerie coincidence. Here we go again. *Intrepid* was forced to return to Pearl Harbor for an additional two weeks while repairs were made.

And because she was being repaired, she might have missed taking part in the largest carrier battle in history. On June 11, less than a week after D-Day, as Allied troops were still fighting to secure their beachhead in Normandy, carrier-based squadrons attacked Saipan in the Mariana Islands.

On June 15, Marines landed on that island. The commander of Japan's Imperial Fleet understood the strategic importance of Saipan. "The fate of the Empire rests upon this single battle," he warned his navy. "Every man is expected to do his utmost." The island was 1,100 miles from the Philippines and 1,400 miles from Japan, within range of the new B-29 Superfortress. If it could be captured, American planes finally could bring the war home to the Japanese.

The Imperial Navy committed 9 carriers, 5 battleships, and more than 500 planes to the battle, while the United States had 16 carriers, 9 battleships, and almost 1,000 airplanes from Task Force 58, including the *Wasp*, *Yorktown*, and *Hornet*. Had *Intrepid* been seaworthy, it is highly probable she would have been in the fight.

During the Battle of the Philippine Sea, almost 400 Japanese planes were destroyed, while Task Force 58 lost 120 aircraft. The fighting was intense; American pilots and naval antiaircraft guns feasted on waves of Japanese attackers. So many enemy planes were shot down in aerial combat that the action eventually became known as The Great Marianas Turkey Shoot.

Almost 4,000 miles away from the fighting, some men aboard the dry-docked *Intrepid* felt wistful, left out of the battle. And every sailor or aviator who had served in the Navy for more than the last few years knew men who were in that battle. They could identify with them. They could see those attacking planes in their nightmares. It was difficult to escape the feeling that they weren't doing their part.

They also knew they would have been in the thick of it if not for the ship's steering problems. And some part of them also understood Americans had been killed in the fighting, and many more would die—while they were safe.

As it turned out, though, their time would come.

Intrepid celebrated its first year in service at sea, sailing towards Eniwetok. "One hundred forty years and six months ago today," Captain Bolger told the crew on that anniversary, "*Intrepid* entered the harbor at Tripoli . . . to carry out what Lord Nelson called 'The most bold and daring act of the age.' . . . In cool courage and fearless bravery. In the spirit of the heroic and undaunted crews of the past, God grant that the accomplishments of our future missions may be additionally 'bold and daring acts of the age.'"

Rick Gaines had a more direct message for his men: "We can't win the war without smelling the smoke of battle. We are on our way again for just that."

Intrepid joined the task force striking the Philippine Islands: Mindanao. Visayas. Luzon. Leyte. While they encountered some opposition, American pilots owned the skies. The enemy was reeling from the attacks. "It seems strange we haven't been attacked," Jake Elefant wrote in his diary, "but I'm thankful for it."

In early October, the fighting paused briefly when the fleet was pummeled by a typhoon. The intense storm ripped seven planes from their moorings and tossed them into the sea. Two of the ship's small launches were carried away.

Catwalks and railings were torn loose. Waves breaking over the flight deck tore up and mangled a small section of it. Gunners tied themselves into their tub positions to keep from being washed overboard.

While the ship was making a sharp turn, it was hit broadside by a massive wall of water; for several seconds, *Intrepid* felt like it might capsize. It was a jolt of instant terror, punctuated by the sounds of loose items smashing against bulkheads. Belowdecks, men held their breath and struggled to keep their balance.

When the storm finally subsided, the ship sailed back into the calm waters of Ulithi. But as they cruised slowly into the lagoon, suddenly, seemingly out of nowhere, a Japanese Betty appeared. Somehow it had evaded radar detection. No one had any idea where it had come from. It materialized as if by magic, and as the crew watched, mystified, it just brushed past the ship and crashed in the lagoon.

It exploded.

It was a very close—and very strange—near miss. To some members of the crew it actually looked as if the pilot was trying to crash his plane into the ship. But they dismissed that thought. That just wasn't possible. Even Japanese pilots weren't that crazy.

What no one realized at that moment was that they might well have just witnessed—and barely escaped with their lives—one of the first suicide attacks of the war at sea. This time they were lucky. This time. But there would be repeated attacks—and the consequences would prove devastating.

As the task force moved closer to Japan, enemy resistance intensified. Land-based enemy planes were now able to reach the fleet. *Intrepid* was in the middle of the action, repulsing attack after attack. Its air group successfully battled enemy attackers while inflicting horrendous damage on Japanese warships. Day after day, sometimes hour after hour, those planes limped back to *Intrepid* pocked with bullet holes, occasionally on fire—almost always to be patched up and put back into the fight. It was a war of attrition, and Japanese forces were being whittled down.

By early October, carrier planes were attacking the islands of Formosa and Okinawa. A massive number of sorties, sometimes more than a thousand a day, devastated what remained of Japan's air forces. The enemy fought back. *Intrepid* successfully dodged several more torpedo attacks. Incredibly, the ship's newfound luck held. A torpedo hit the ship at a sharp angle, and rather than penetrating the hull, it literally bounced off, then exploded harmlessly.

Luck.

On October 20, General Douglas MacArthur fulfilled the promise he had so famously made—"I shall return"—when the Japanese had captured the Philippines. Slightly more than two and a half years later, he returned, triumphantly walking through the surf onto Leyte Island. Twice. The second time for reporters and photographers who missed it the first time.

The Battle of Leyte Gulf would become the largest naval battle in history. More than 300 Navy ships of every type fought about 75 Japanese ships. During the fighting, *Intrepid* celebrated the 7,000th landing on its flight deck as well as the 1,000th successful launch from its catapults. On February 25, bombers and fighters from the ship's air wing help sink two Japanese battleships and two cruisers.

That afternoon, in one of those inexplicable events that take place in wartime, *Intrepid* recovered a pilot and gunner who had been shot down and somehow managed to get back to fleet—in a Japanese sailboat.

The Japanese were losing the war. In desperation, the Imperial air corps initiated a new and terrifying tactic. On October 25, they launched the first wave of flying bombs, stripped-down airplanes whose pilots sacrificed themselves by crashing their planes into American ships.

Admiral Tom Sprague's task group, designated Taffy One, was the first to encounter them. A Zero dove on the escort carrier *Santee*, firing its guns into the flight deck. There was nothing unusual about that. But what happened next was astonishing. Rather than pulling up and racing away to safety, the plane continued right into the ship.

Sixteen sailors died instantly. The crew was stunned; the pilot had committed suicide. Any doubts that this was intentional were erased minutes later when a second suicide pilot crashed his plane into Sprague's flagship, *Suwannee*. Several other suicide planes were shot down, but another kamikaze struck Sprague's ship the next day, causing casualties, severe damage, and fires that burned for hours.

A new and terrifying word had entered the English language: *kamikaze*. It translated to mean *heavenly wind* or *divine wind*. Suddenly, that single plane that had nearly slammed into *Intrepid* in Ulithi lagoon weeks earlier took on a darker, foreboding meaning.

The luck that had protected the ship that day ran out on October 29. That morning, the task force shot down a dozen Japanese planes. But the enemy was relentless. In midafternoon, 14 more Japanese aircraft attacked. One of them, an older model Zero, flew past *Intrepid*'s stern. Rather than heading away from the ship, it climbed high into the sky. Then, at the apex of its ascent, it turned and dived back towards the ship.

All of the ship's antiaircraft guns—the 20mm, the 40mm, the booming 5-inchers—opened fire. The plane kept coming. It was hit. Its left wing was blown off. It began spiraling wildly. But still, it came down, straight down. The plane barely missed the flight deck, instead slamming into gun tub #10.

Gun tub #10 was manned by Black steward's mates. In the segregated Navy, Black sailors aboard combat ships served in the officer's mess or cleaned officer's staterooms—but they also could volunteer for secondary duty as gunners. #10 was commanded by 22-year-old Mexican American gunner's mate Alfonso Chavarrias, who had survived the sinking of the *Lexington* in the Coral Sea. As the plane whirled directly down towards them, while other gun crews scrambled to safety the men in #10 heroically remained in position. They never stopped firing.

The kamikaze's remaining wing ripped through the gun tub. Six men were killed instantly. Fuel from the plane washed over the tub and burst into flames. Ammunition began exploding. Another dozen men were trapped in the inferno. Incredibly, their shipmates raced right into the fire, pulling out survivors without concern for their own safety. Seaman Al Brouseau lay down on top of a burning crewmate, using his own body to extinguish the flames. Nineteen-year-old Steward's Mate Alonzo Swann ignored his own serious burns to rescue several shipmates. Another man grabbed the 20mm ammunition magazine that was feeding the guns and tossed it over the side. It was bedlam, but no one panicked. They risked their own lives. They saved lives. By staying at their post they may have saved the ship.

The remains of the enemy plane fell into the sea.

Four more men died of their injuries in the next few hours. Several more men were hospitalized with second-degree burns.

Intrepid had become the first of America's fast carriers to be hit by a kamikaze.

Only hours after the attack, a burial service was held for the heroes of gun tub #10. Their bodies were given to the sea. But in the middle of this solemn service, radar picked up another wave of attackers. The men scrambled to their battle stations. The kamikazes had come back. In the next 22 minutes, the task force shot down seven more enemy planes.

And then the funeral service resumed.

Although six of the survivors were told they would receive the Navy Cross, the Navy's highest award for valor, they instead were awarded the Bronze Star. There were whispers that they were denied that honor because of their race. That slight would be rectified six decades later, after Swann filed suit in federal court when Chavarrias and Alonzo Swann Jr. finally received Navy's highest honor.

The men who crewed those tubs knew how vulnerable they were. Captain Sprague's aide, Tony Zollo, was also a gunner. As he wrote, "I was always thinking and looking around and asking myself what if this or that happens. I had a coil of rope hanging in the ready room close to the hatch. Should I ever be unable to get out of the tub it was my intention to tie the rope to the gun mount and go over the side and into the water. I always had a life preserver handy for this same reason."

Unfortunately, this attack was only a prelude. On November 25, *Intrepid* was 60 miles off the coast of Luzon. Its planes were attacking "The Tokyo Express," the Japanese transports carrying reinforcement to the Philippines. The kamikazes returned at noon. "All hell broke loose," Elefant wrote. There were so many enemy planes that radar screens looked like active beehives. The entire task force opened fire with everything they had. It wasn't enough.

A Japanese dive-bomber targeted the carrier *Hancock*. Seconds before impact, the ship's gunners blew up the plane, but the flaming debris smashed into two fully fueled planes on the flight deck. A huge ball of fire erupted. The deck was engulfed in massive flames.

Intrepid's crew watched in horror as black smoke from *Hancock*'s deck darkened the sky. There was nothing they could do to help. Instead, they took one deep breath, then got ready to fight the next wave. Incredibly, though, the enemy seemed to have disappeared. They were gone.

Intrepid resumed launching and recovering the planes of Air Group 6.

Minutes passed. In the command center, the radar men hunched over their screens. The enemy was out there somewhere. The guess was, they were regrouping for a larger attack.

They waited. No one took their eyes off their screens.

The kamikazes came back at 1252. Another massive wave. The enemy was throwing everything it had at the task force. Planes attacked from every direction. *Intrepid*'s radar picked up two Zeros at 8,000 feet astern—heading directly for the ship. Its gunners put up a wall of fire. The kamikazes dropped down to 50 feet. One of the attackers was hit about 1,500 yards out, but the second pilot swerved, juked, and kept coming. "He was so close that I knew we were going to get hit," Elefant wrote. "We took cover. Just then I felt the ship shudder and I knew the pilot had crashed on our flight deck with his bomb."

The kamikaze smashed through the wooden flight deck into a vacant ready room. Thirty-two men in an adjacent compartment died in the explosion, most of them radar men waiting to go on duty. Ray Stone had been in there. Only minutes earlier he had stepped outside onto a walkway—and became one of the few survivors from his division.

Once again, men raced heroically into the fires. Oily black smoke spewing from the ship made it a big target for more kamikazes. The smoke also made it almost impossible for Intrepid's gunners to see attacking planes. In some cases, they fired blindly into the smoke. They needed some good luck.

They didn't get it. Minutes later, a second kamikaze hit the already wounded ship. This plane slid along the flight deck, igniting fires while its 500-pound bomb crashed into the hangar deck and detonated.

When the crew saw the kamikaze coming directly at them, Elefant wrote, "everyone took shelter and once again we felt another shudder. When we came out the ship was just enveloped in smoke. Pieces of both the . . . planes were strewn all over the flight deck. The body of one of the enemy pilots had slid up the flight deck about 400 feet from where he had crashed, and so did his engine. Everyone took to fighting the fire and things looked really bad."

Admiral Halsey watched from his flagship, the *New Jersey.* "An instant after *Intrepid* was hit she was wrapped in flames," he later recalled. "Blazing gasoline cascaded down her sides, explosions rocked her; then oily black smoke, rising thousands of feet, hid everything but her bow."

They were losing the ship. The hangar deck was engulfed in flames. Planes began exploding, firing off their ammunition, which riddled bulkheads. Men hit the floor or ran for their lives. In minutes, 22 planes were destroyed. Billowing smoke filled the forward engine room, which was on the verge of being abandoned. Rumors spread quickly: *prepare to abandon ship.*

Instead, they fought back. While crews were fighting the fires, the seriously wounded were laid out on a safe area of the flight deck for emergency treatment. Inside the smoke-filled radar room, men got down on the floor, filled their lungs with air, then stood up and watched their screens until the smoke finally overwhelmed them. When they could only see inches in front of them, it was time to get out. They held hands and groped for the ladder, barely escaping.

The entire task force was under attack. The *Essex* was hit. The *Cabot* was hit. *Hancock* was rocked by more explosions. The battleships *Iowa* and *New Jersey* moved in as close as possible to *Hancock* so their gunners could defend the burning ship.

It would take hours before the fires raging through *Intrepid* were brought under control. "Besides damage to the ship," Elefant concluded his notes, "we lost many of our shipmates. The totals being 64 dead, 85 wounded and 10 missing. We secured around 1830 [hours], a very tired and weary group of men, but thankful that most of us were still alive."

The final toll was 69 dead, at least 150 men wounded. Gordon Keith and several assistants once again were kept busy preparing canvas body bags. The dead were given to the sea the next morning.

Intrepid's flight deck had been gutted, putting the ship out of action. It returned to Ulithi for emergency repairs.

The oddities of war continued. As the wreckage was still being cleared, a Japanese pilot who had been shot down and captured was put aboard the ship. Ironically, being shot down had probably saved his life. His only injury was a broken arm, suffered when his bullet-riddled plane hit the water. There were a lot of men on the ship who had lost buddies and would have liked a shot at the prisoner, but he was locked in sick bay and carefully guarded.

Intrepid returned to Hunter's Point in late December 1944. Three months later, with a new captain, Giles E. Short, and a new air group equipped with additional fighters to meet the threat from kamikazes, she was part of a massive task force gathering to begin the final attack on Japan.

The Empire of the Rising Sun was fighting for its existence. It committed all its remaining resources to the battle. During the battle for the outer island of Okinawa, almost 900 enemy planes were sent to attack the task force, including at least 350 kamikazes.

On March 17, as *Intrepid*'s air group was bombing and strafing enemy airfields, a Japanese bomber was shot down only 150 feet from the ship, so close that fragments rained onto the hangar deck and ignited a fire. The now veteran crew was able to extinguish the fires in less than an hour.

A day later, the *Wasp* was hit, killing 101 men. Hundreds more died when two bombs crashed through the *Franklin*'s flight deck. On April 16, a total of 300 enemy planes attacked the task force, half of them kamikazes. Few people even noticed the date: the 16th. But they would never forget it.

Two suicide planes targeted *Intrepid*. One of them was shot down about 1,000 yards away, but the second plane weaved through blistering fire and crashed into the flight deck. Its 500-pound bomb tore through that deck and exploded on the hangar deck. Eight crewmen were killed, 21 more were wounded, and 40 planes were destroyed. While the crew were fighting raging fires, two Zeros dropped bombs that missed the ship by less than 100 yards.

The extensive damage put the ship out of the battle, forcing her to once again return to San Francisco for repairs. Months later, on August 15, 1945, after participating in the raids on Wake Island *Intrepid* was moored at Eniwetok when Emperor Hirohito announced his nation's unconditional surrender.

The war was over. Almost. During the next few weeks, the ship participated in cleanup operations in Korea and China. By the end of combat operations, *Intrepid* was credited with sinking 89 ships and downing more than 660 enemy planes. She had been hit by kamikazes four times. And then she went home . . .

Several years later, the ship's cruise book attempted to sum up its wartime service. "The *Intrepid* earned many nicknames during the war . . ." it began. "She was called the 'Evil I' because of her propensity to collect Japanese torpedoes, bombs and Kamikazes, which she did more often than any other carrier that remained afloat. But more than any nickname, her own name, the *Intrepid*, best described her behavior throughout the war. She was bombed, torpedoed, strafed and crashed by Kamikazes, she was ripped open, burned and twisted; she lost a great many men on her decks and in the air but she always came back and fought again, boldly, undaunted, fearlessly and courageously, again and again and again . . .

"Every time the Japanese sighted her it was as though a ghost had appeared. They had reported her sunk several times, yet it seemed she was always back to hurt them . . . She would not die . . . She would not quit. In the end it was the *Intrepid* that sat quietly in Tokyo Bay . . ."

After leaving the *Intrepid*, Admiral Sprague's Carrier Division 22 played an important role in capturing Saipan and Guam. Having already received the Legion of Merit, he was awarded a Gold Star for his work in planning the largest amphibious operation of the entire war, the invasion of Leyte. Months later he was honored with the Navy Cross "For extraordinary heroism . . . in the support of landings on a heavily defended enemy-held island base . . . subjected to bombardment, torpedo attacks and suicide dive bombing attacks each of the units of his command performed in an outstanding manner . . . This attack was a major element in turning back a powerful Task Force of the Japanese Fleet . . . A situation replete with danger was turned into a brilliant victory."

Rear Admiral Thomas Sprague ended the war with a chest full of medals and ribbons; in 1943 he had taken command of a new ship still being fitted out in Virginia with an inexperienced, untested crew, transformed it into a potent weapon, and within another year was in command of a task force inflicting significant damage on major Japanese cities.

After the war, he served as head of the Navy's Bureau of Personnel. Then, in the early 1950s, he took command of the

Pacific Fleet's Air Force as it fought the communist invasion of South Korea. He retired in 1952 after leading the Navy's First Task Fleet. His extraordinary five-decade career had spanned the very beginnings of naval aviation, from biplanes propelled off a houseboat to squadrons of jet fighters launched from the decks of carriers off the coast of Korea.

Three years later, he was briefly recalled to active duty to assist the Department of Defense in renegotiating an agreement for the continued presence of American forces in the Philippines.

In the years following the war, the incredible story of the sail that saved the *Intrepid* grew to legendary proportions. For people learning about it for the first time, it seemed like one of those impossible to believe, mythical stories. But Tom Sprague always took great pride in his part of it, including prominent mention of it in his official Navy biography: "During the night after the first raid, *Intrepid* was attacked by a Japanese torpedo plane and struck by a torpedo, the explosion jamming her rudder and destroying the steering engines and flooding the after end of the ship. He ordered a sail rigged to assist in steering control, headed the ship clear of the battle area and returning 6000 miles to San Francisco for repairs."

And in his 1972 obituary, the *Navy Times* wrote, "Admiral Sprague first gained recognition in 1944 when he rigged a sail on the forecastle of the aircraft carrier *Intrepid* to help steer the vessel to Pearl Harbor after she was attacked by Japanese torpedo planes during the battle for Truk."

Philip Reynolds, who received an official commendation for his efforts in creating the sail, retired in 1954. After Japan's

surrender, he was given his command of the attack transport
USS *Calvert*, which participated in Operation Magic Carpet,
supporting and transporting occupying troops in Japan and
parts of China back to the United States.

Following that, he served in several technical positions,
from the inspector of naval machinery at General Motors
to assistant chief of staff for personnel in the Ninth Naval
District. Upon his retirement, the secretary of the Navy
wrote, "You have achieved an excellent service reputation
for thoroughness, ingenuity and intelligent administration."

Ingenuity.

In September 1944, Richard Kenna Gaines, who had served
as *Intrepid*'s XO since it was commissioned, became deputy chief
of staff of the Navy's Air Technical Training Center. After some
additional training in Pensacola, he took command of the escort
carrier *Salerno Bay*, eventually returning to Pensacola in 1948
to take charge of the Naval Air Station—literally two decades
since he had earned his wings there.

During the Korean War, he was promoted to commodore
and eventually became the chief of staff to the chairman of
the US Mission's Military Staff Committee at the United
Nations. Rick Gaines retired from the Navy in 1955.

Frank Johnson had left *Intrepid* a month before Gaines, in
August 1944. Johnson was one of the experienced, skilled
veterans who kept the Navy on an even keel. He spent the
last year of the war on the staff of the US Naval Training and
Distribution Center in Shoemaker, California. Following the
Japanese surrender, he transferred to the light cruiser *Spring-
field*, which returned to the Marianas, shuttling between Saipan
and Guam. He retired as a chief boson's mate in late 1946.

Sprague, Reynolds, and Gaines were academy grads and Navy lifers, and Johnson was a long-time veteran, but "Flash" Gordon Keith had enlisted at least partially to get out of his small town and "see the world." He saw a lot more of it than he might had expected, having seen combat in nine different major operations—earning more than a dozen awards and honors. Like millions of American veterans, in 1946 he returned to civilian life. But then a strange thing happened. After working in a factory for two years in Akron, Ohio, he realized he missed the service. Whatever it was—the camaraderie, the opportunity, the structure—he missed it. So he enlisted in the newly created US Air Force. He spent the next 14 years in Air-Sea Rescue both overseas and domestically, retiring from the Air Force as a master sergeant.

Then he became a park ranger in Florida.

Ray Stone was one of several plank owners who served on *Intrepid* until the end of the war, surviving all four kamikaze hits and the infamous torpedoing. After being discharged in late 1945, he attended the Art Students League under the GI Bill, eventually becoming a creative director and president of New York's SSK&F advertising agency. His diary, *"My Ship!"* which detailed his two years aboard *Intrepid*, was published in 2003.

As the Navy trimmed down its fighting fleet after the war, *Intrepid* waited patiently in reserve. In 1952 the ship was extensively modernized to enable it to carry jet aircraft and again four years later, when an angled flight deck was installed and the fo'c'sle, where the sail had once flown, was permanently enclosed. The introduction of jet planes had erased the need to warm up planes before bringing them up to the flight deck.

Unlike the piston engines used in World War II aircraft, jet engines require considerably less time to warm up. In addition, the increased use of catapults cut down the time needed to launch aircraft.

The remodeled, refurbished ship served multiple purposes as America entered the space age. In May 1962, *Intrepid* recovered astronaut Scott Carpenter, the second American to orbit the earth. Three years later, the ship plucked Gemini 3 astronauts Virgil "Gus" Grissom and John Young and their capsule out of the Atlantic after they overshot their planned landing area by more than 50 miles.

Seven months after that, she went back to war, taking up station in the Gulf of Tonkin, off the coast of Vietnam. During three tours between 1966 and 1969, its planes flew thousands of sorties over both North and South Vietnam and later Laos. In a small twist of fate, in July 1967, the ship entered dry dock to replace two damaged propellers—in Yokosuka, Japan.

Vietnam was a different type of war. The ship faced little danger from enemy airplanes, surface ships, or submarines, but its air group was confronted by highly accurate surface-to-air missiles that took a substantial toll.

While in combat, the now fully enclosed *Intrepid* managed to catapult 15 fully armed jet aircraft off the deck in 7 minutes, with an incredible 26 seconds between launches.

After completing its final tour in Vietnam, the ship sailed home. By 1970 she was the Navy's oldest aircraft carrier still in fleet operation. And the ship was showing its age. Although it had been continually updated, it was becoming more and more difficult to install modern technology on its World War II platform. Finally, in 1973 the Navy decided to put her in mothballs—take her out of active service. All the still usable bits and pieces were removed, and *Intrepid* essentially was put in a permanent parking lot. On May 15, 1974, months after 30 years in service, *Intrepid* was decommissioned.

There was no practical use and little value in an old, rusting aircraft carrier. It seemed only a matter of time before *Intrepid* was scrapped. But there were people who wanted to save the ship, to honor its gallant service. Among the wildest ideas was welding two carriers bow to bow to create a short takeoff and landing runway in New York's Hudson River.

In the early 1970s, New Yorker Michael Piccola suggested turning one of the nation's remaining World War II carriers into a museum to showcase aviation history. Eventually another prominent New Yorker, Zachery Fisher, who had been successful in construction and real estate and had become a leader in supporting veterans' causes, spearheaded the effort. The Intrepid Museum Foundation was created in 1979, and the Intrepid Sea, Air and Space Museum opened on the west side of Manhattan in August 1982.

Since then, the ship and the museum have been extensively renovated to enable them to display an array of airplanes, memorabilia, and interactive experiences. After a sluggish start, the museum has grown to become one of New York's most popular attractions, visited annually by more than 1 million people.

Occasionally visitors explore the now enclosed forecastle, which has been restored to its historic appearance. There isn't much to see there, just massive anchor chains and related equipment that will never be used again. A curving gray steel bulkhead encloses the area. While there is audio of anchors being dropped and crew members describing the process, visitors to that area have to envision what it must have been like in late February 1944 when the area was open and it was being battered by high winds and waves while Tom Sprague, up on the bridge, fought to control his ship.

They have to close their eyes and imagine what it must have felt like to be on *Intrepid* as the out-of-control ship spun wildly through the night, barely missing a catastrophic collision with the *Essex*.

There is a small photo of the sail placed there. It's taken from the side and shows only a small portion of it rigged. But people have to dig deep into their minds to visualize what the storied sail must have looked like as it caught and held back the winds to enable *Intrepid* to get home.

★ ★ ★ ★ ★

ACKNOWLEDGMENTS

We have been very fortunate while working on this book to have had the invaluable assistance of several people.

The entire staff of the Intrepid Sea, Air and Space Museum embraced and enhanced our effort every step of the way. We would like to especially thank the museum's president Susan Marenoff-Zausner, Head Curator Jessica Williams who so graciously did so much so often, and her always smiling assistant Danielle Swanson. The Intrepid Museum serves as an astonishing tribute to the men and women of America's Navy and Air Force (and submariners) and should be a mandatory stop on a visit to the city. If you haven't been there, you should go!

We also have enjoyed support from several people associated with the Navy in our quest to tell this story, and among them are Admiral (retired) Samuel J. Cox, Alan Baribeau and Evan Wilson.

Our chief researcher, Ann Trevor (atrevor10@gmail.com), was wonderful to work with. In addition to being responsive, she is creative, diligent, thorough and timely, everything we could want as we explored this world. She worked with the equally enthusiastic, responsive and capable Lori Miller (redbirdresearch.gmail.com) who poured through and copied thousands of documents without ever losing her joy or curiosity. We are happy to recommend both Ann and Lori for any military research.

In researching and writing this book we have come to greatly appreciate and admire the men and women who served on this gallant ship in her many guises, and salute you all for the history you created. We also have been in touch with the families of several Intrepid plank holders, who have been forthcoming in their memories and graciously allowed us the use of their relatives materials. In particular, we are grateful to Andrea Richards, David deMarco, Stuart Elefant, Norah Spear, Anthony Zollo Jr. and Lloyd Keith. We hope they enjoyed this process as much as we did.

We remain grateful to our agent, Frank Weimann, Vice President of Folio, who put us in the hands of one of the finest publishers in the entire industry, Peter Joseph. Without the two of them and the many fine people at Hanover Square Press—especially Eden Railsback and Leah Morse—this book would not exist. Thank you.

MONTEL WILLIAMS would also like to acknowledge:

I am sincerely grateful to the remarkable individuals who contributed to making this book a reality. First and foremost, my heartfelt appreciation goes to my talented coauthor, David Fisher. Collaborating with you has been an honor and a privilege, and I hope it marks the start of many future endeavors together. Your unparalleled skill and dedication have enriched this project, and I feel fortunate to have shared this experience with you as we brought the heroic story of *The Sailing of the Intrepid* to life.

A special acknowledgment is due to my dear friend Ken Fisher. Your steadfast support—whether through your invaluable foreword or granting access to the Intrepid Air, Sea and Space Museum archives—has been truly extraordinary. Your family's unwavering dedication to supporting our military personnel, veterans, and the preservation of military history deeply inspires and humbles me. I am also proud to serve alongside Ken as a member of the Fisher House Foundation Board of Trustees, where we work tirelessly to support military families and veterans in need.

I am also profoundly honored to recognize Secretary of the Navy Carlos Del Toro. Witnessing your enduring service to our nation has been a privilege over the years. Your enthusiasm for this pivotal chapter in Navy history and your contribution of a thoughtful introduction are deeply appreciated. Thank you for your invaluable support.

I extend my utmost gratitude to Victor Minella, Deputy Under Secretary of the Navy (Intelligence and Security), for his ongoing encouragement throughout the development of this book. Additionally, I would like to thank RADM Samuel J. Cox, Director of the Naval History and Heritage Command, for his instrumental role in preserving the proud legacy of our Navy. Your insights and expertise have been key to ensuring the historical accuracy and depth of *The Sailing of the Intrepid*. Thank you for championing naval history with such unwavering passion and commitment.

To my dedicated team, my extended family, I owe my deepest appreciation. Melanie McLaughlin, my manager and business partner of more than 35 years, your hard work, wisdom, and unshakable loyalty have been a constant source of support and strength. I am endlessly thankful for your guidance and steadfast commitment.

To Jonathan Franks, my senior advisor and publicist of more than 15 years, your partnership has been both essential and profoundly meaningful. Our collaborative mission to bring home wrongfully detained veterans stands as critical work I am honored to perform alongside you. I look forward to continuing this important endeavor.

To Keith McLaughlin—podcast producer, editor, marketer, and all-around production powerhouse—your exceptional dedication, unparalleled expertise, and friendship have been indispensable. Your tireless efforts make it possible for me to do what I do, and I am truly grateful.

My heartfelt thanks also go to my incredible partners at Brandstar Studios and Production, whose vision and efforts have been vital to the success of our *Military Makeover with Montel* series. Your creativity and steadfast commitment to connecting with and uplifting our veteran community inspire me every day. Working together to transform lives and offer hope to those who have given so much to our nation is deeply meaningful. Creating each episode with such a passionate team reinforces our shared mission of making a positive impact.

Lastly, I want to honor Dr. Frank Bourke. Your tireless dedication to developing groundbreaking treatments for post-traumatic stress disorder, particularly the Reconsolidation of Traumatic Memories Protocol, is a daily source of inspiration.

It is a privilege to support the Research & Recognition Project and contribute to this life-changing work for our veterans and service members.

To everyone who has played a part in this project, I express my profound gratitude for your contributions and belief in this endeavor. *The Sailing of the Intrepid* would not have been possible without each of you. Thank you from the bottom of my heart.

DAVID FISHER would also like to acknowledge:

What a great voyage this has been, and I have been amazingly fortunate to have embarked on it with my co-author Montel Williams. There is no one more proud of his association with the United States Navy and Marine Corps and all of the men and women who served this country than Montel. He has made sure at every opportunity that their service was acknowledged and praised—and that we got this story right. It's a great treat to work with him. I appreciate his hard work, his expertise, his dedication and his problem solving ability and look forward to a long association.

Making this process so much easier was Montel's assistant, Melanie McLaughlin, president of Montel's companies and just an all-around terrific person to work with. When something needed to be done, and done well, Mel did it. I hope she knows how much I appreciate her presence and her professionalism.

And although I am no relation to Ken Fisher (sigh!) I also appreciate his enthusiastic support from an idea to the story in these pages.

I was also extremely lucky to have had the expert advice of my friends and former submariners Captain John McGunnigle and John Ranelli, who keen eyes helped us find and correct the flaws in the drafts. And I strongly suggest you read their forthcoming book, *Submarine Close.*

And finally, as always, my endless love and gratitude for my personal rudder, my wife, Laura, who maintains our course and does everything necessary to ensure a safe voyage as she has done now for 25 years. What a lucky man I am. Our sons, Taylor and Beau, also did whatever was necessary to help, as did our loving Chihuahua, Willow Bay, who often sat with me as we filled blank pages.

BIBLIOGRAPHY

Celander, Lars, *How Carriers Fought: Carrier Operations in World War II.* Havertown, Pennsylvania: 2020

Coyne, E., *Experiences Aboard Intrepid During WWII.* 2023

Faltum, Andrew, *Aircraft Carrier Intrepid.* Annapolis, Maryland: Naval Institute Press, 2022

Faltum, Andrew, *The Essex Aircraft Carriers.* Baltimore, Maryland: The Nautical & Aviation Publishing Company of America, 1996

Fold 3/military records, *Ancestry.com*

Friedman, Norman, *U.S. Aircraft Carriers, Revised Edition: An Illustrated Design History.* Annapolis, Maryland: Naval Institute Press, 2022

Gilbert, Martin, *The Second World War: A Complete History.* New York, New York: Henry Holt & Company, 1989

Hood, Jean (Editor), *Carrier: A Century of First-Hand Accounts of Naval Operations in War and Peace*. London, United Kingdom: Conway Books, 2010

Intrepid Cruise Book, 1943–1945, *www.navysite.de/cruisebooks /cv11-45/014.htm*

McNitt, Robert W., *Sailing at the U.S. Naval Academy: An Illustrated History*. Annapolis, Maryland: Naval Institute Press, 1966

Miller, Max, *Carrier!: Life Aboard a World War II Aircraft Carrier*. Santa Monica, California: Thunderbolt Books, 2019

Naval Damage Control Training Center, *Handbook of Damage Control*. New York, New York: New York Training, Bureau of Naval Personnel, 1945 (Restored Copy by 4th Watch Publishing: USGOVPUB.com, November 27, 2021)

Naval History and Heritage Command, *www.history.navy.mil*

Office of Deputy Chief of Naval Operations (Air), *Our Flying Navy*. New York, New York: The Macmillan Company, 1944

Oral histories, *Intrepidmuseum.org/resources*

Reynolds, Clark, *The Carrier War*. Alexandria, Virginia: Time-Life Books, 1982

Richard L. Montfort diary, April 1943–May 1944, *Intrepid museum.org*

Roberts, John, *The Aircraft Carrier Intrepid: Anatomy of the Ship.* Annapolis, Maryland: Naval Institute Press, 1982

Stone, Raymond T., *"My Ship!": The U.S.S. Intrepid.* South Salem, New York: G.P. Books, 2003

Stuart Elefant diary, August 1943–June 1944, *Intrepidmuseum.org*

The National Archives, Washington, D.C., *www.archives.gov /research*

Toll, Ian W., *Six Frigates: The Epic History of the Founding of the U.S. Navy.* New York, New York: W.W. Norton & Company, 2006

United States Naval Academy, *The Lucky Bag, 1918.* Reprinted: London, United Kingdom: Forgotten Books, 2018

United States Naval Academy, *The Lucky Bag, 1921.* Reprinted: London, United Kingdom: Forgotten Books, 2018

Various American newspapers, 1910–1945, *Newspapers.com*

White, Bill, and Gandt, Robert, *Intrepid: The Epic Story of America's Most Legendary Warship.* New York, New York: Broadway Books, 2008

Wooldridge, E.T. (Editor), *Carrier Warfare in the Pacific: An Oral History Collection.* Washington, DC: Smithsonian Institution Press, 1993

Zollo, Anthony F., Sr., *USS Intrepid (50th Anniversary): The "Fighting I" Illustrated History*. Paducah, Kentucky: Turner Publishing Company, 1993

Zollo, Anthony F., Sr., *USS Intrepid CV-11 Day by Day: Accounts of the Carrier Intrepid in World War II*. Virginia Beach, Virginia: The Donning Company Publishers, 2001

INDEX